MEN
TO MATCH
OUR
MOUNTAINS

JAY LAWSON

www.pronghornpress.org

*This book is dedicated to
my good friend and mentor,
Cal King, who encouraged me
to write these stories.*

Table of Contents

Introduction.....11

1 Ramul Dvarishkis.....17
   A Man of the Mountains

2 Max Wilde.....25
   A "Wild" Life for a Legend Named Wilde

3 Ned Frost.....37
   Inventing the Wilderness Hunt

4 Ernie Faler.....45
   Wyoming's Greatest Sheep Hunter

5 David Prager.....53
   Latter-Day Mountain Man

6 Mel Stonehouse.....61
   Last of the Old Time Cowboy Hunters

7 Leonard "Curly" Corbin.....73
   Wyoming's Hunting Lumberjack

8 Sam Young Jr. 85
   Legendary Hunter of the Greys River

9 Albert Nelson.....97
   Hunter, Outdoorsman, and Our First Game Warden

10 Anson Eddy.....109
    A Life in the Wilderness

11 Mary Price.....119
    A Woman to Match Both Men and Mountains

12 Kenny Martin.....129
    The Cowboy Game Warden

13 John Aeschbach.....141
    Guardian of Little Horn Canyon

14 Don Bell.....149
    Recollections of a Rodeo Cowboy and Big Game Hunter

15 Cal King......159
    Game Warden, Biologist, Scholar

16 Joe and Mary Back.....171
    The Cowboy Meets a Lady

17 S.N. Leek......183
    Father of the Elk

18 D.C. Nowlin.....193
    Frontier Peace Officer and Pioneer Conservationist

19 James R. Simon.....203
    Biologist and Cinematographer

20 Charles J. Belden.....215
    Cowboy Photographer

21 Hans Kleiber.....225
    Forest Ranger and Artist of the Big Horns

22 James W. Spriggs.....237
    Restoring Wyoming's Wildlife

23 Floyd Blunt.....247
    Rapport with the Wild

24 Leone Olds.....261
    The French Trapper's Daughter

25 Snook Moore.....271
    Life as Wilderness Adventure

26 Brida Gafford.....283
    Wyoming's World Champion Cowgirl

27 Henry and Frances Purvis.....291
    Dwellers of the Thorofare

In Conclusion.....299

About the Author.....303

Wyoming Outdoor Timeline.....305

The Wildlife Heritage Foundation of Wyoming.....315

Introduction

Given Wyoming's colorful frontier history, it is little wonder the historical focus has been on the 1800s. The mountain men held the majority of their rendezvous here and many of the major clashes between Indians and cavalry took place in our state. With its failed treaties and the emanation of the Oregon and Bozeman Trails, Fort Laramie could be considered the epicenter of western expansion. Then came the open range cattle industry and its Cheyenne Club, the war on Powder River, the Hole-in-the-Wall Gang, and the list goes on. It is almost as though nothing beyond 1890 could measure up. Consequently, the early twentieth century has received inadequate attention.

Growing up in Wyoming during the 1950s and 60s, I became enthralled at an early age with the old-timers who were born in the horseback era and lived in a time when the central Rocky Mountains were largely unoccupied and undeveloped. Though elderly and often nondescript in appearance, many of them had fascinating life histories to share if someone expressed an interest and would simply listen.

My first lesson in discovering the past was the interaction I had with an old cowboy named Ted Cardwell. He would have been just another senior citizen to most kids, but his collection of old rifles, pistols and knives told me there had been adventure in his early years.

Through patient listening I would discover he had been a cowboy, homesteader and government hunter at different times in his life. He trapped the last wolves in the Shirley Mountains and helped his father shoot wagonloads of wild game to feed work crews constructing Pathfinder Dam on the North Platte River. As a young cowboy, he actually packed the Colt six shooters that now lay in an antique cabinet in his apartment. Photos of Ted were rare but one that sticks in my mind is him sitting in front of a sod-roofed cabin he had constructed in the Bates Hole country, his broad-brimmed cowboy hat tilted back in the jaunty fashion of that era.

Ted would often haul me around in his old truck and we would eventually end up at a ranch his relatives owned where we would shoot his classic guns. My favorite was a Savage rifle in .22 High Power, one of the earliest guns developed for predator hunting. Ted carried that rifle as a government hunter, and his attachment to it was obvious. Hunting predators on horseback was arduous work, but he had thrived on it. To a young boy like myself, his stories were thrilling, but they also became lessons in history and inspired my interest in his generation.

When I think back on Ted Cardwell, the thing I remember most is what a gentleman he was. He always had a kind word for you, his standard greeting being, "How you been, kid?" and he parted company with the farewell, "Take your time goin', but hurry back." Truly a classic Western character.

Another old-timer I became friends with was Homer Clark. Like Ted, he homesteaded along Bates Creek in central Wyoming, and had done his share of cowboying. He also had a collection of early Winchester guns he used in his younger days which seemed to connect him to the first years of twentieth century Wyoming.

Homer loved to fish and, when he became too elderly to drive, I would pack him up and head to one of his favorite haunts. Fishing provided the perfect opportunity to visit at length about the early days; stories of his mother's experience with Indians or the many hunting tales from the era when shooting a mule deer or antelope was serious business if there was going to be food on the table. These were wonderful outings and they again fueled my interest in the neglected history of that era.

Becoming a game warden realized all of my career ambitions, but it also provided opportunities to meet many of the most delightful outdoor characters in Wyoming. They are the people you will meet in this book. Some I met out in the hills, others I knew by reputation and sought them out. Tape recording did not sit well with most of them, so I simply jotted abbreviated notes on my small pocket notepad for future reference.

The inspiration to actually write these life histories came in several forms. The first was my reading of Louis L'Amour's autobiography, *Education of a Wandering Man*. The genesis of his Western novels had been the frontier veterans still living when he was a young man traveling through the West. There were stories everywhere, and he captured them in his writing; that foundation in real-world events and personalities set his Westerns apart from pure fiction.

The paintings of James Bama also made me realize that the history of these unique people had to be preserved. Bama gave up a career in commercial art and moved from New York to Wyoming in mid-career. He soon became intrigued by the colorful old-timers around Cody and was befriended by a number of them. The portraits he produced captured their real Western personas and preserved history that was soon to be lost.

When I finally met James Bama, it struck me how much he embodied the personality traits of many of the Westerners he had painted—a true gentleman with a spark in his eye and a keen sense of humor.

Retired wildlife biologist Cal King knew I had been interviewing some of the old cowboys and hunters, and he urged me to write about them. During the 1960s, Cal sought out many of the early trappers and wolf hunters in preparation for a book on the history of wildlife in the Big Horn Basin. Among the characters he interviewed was "High Power" Williams, who gained fame when he tracked down both the

Custer Wolf and the Spirit Rock Wolf. Those were the last of the lone wolves that were big livestock killers. Cal's writing preserved that history, and he encouraged me to do the same.

By writing this collection of biographies, I hope to save a small piece of Wyoming's past that is quickly disappearing. My first recollections were of men I had known, hence the title *Men to Match our Mountains*; however, I later discovered several intriguing outdoor women, whom I've included. The times you will read about are long past and many of the old-timers I interviewed have left us since I began this project, but their fascinating lives will not be forgotten.

Ramul Dvarishkis (right) operated a one-man outfitting business for years in northwest Wyoming. He packed everything in, set up camp and wrangled horses, guided hunters and cooked meals. Still living in Thermopolis, Dvarishkis guided his last successful client when he was 81.
Photo courtesy of Jessie Dvarishkis.

1

Ramul Dvarishkis
A Man of the Mountains

By the end of the nineteenth century, a significant portion of Wyoming's big game resource had been extirpated by market hunting and unregulated shooting by settlers. Few antelope remained, deer were scarce and elk had been eliminated in many mountain ranges. Consequently, the first decades of the twentieth century saw most areas closed to hunting or open on a very limited basis.

Exceptions to this rather bleak period in our hunting history were the wilderness horseback hunts in the most remote portions of western Wyoming. This was the last bastion of big game, and the hunting trips that took place during this period were probably the greatest adventures since the free trapper and mountain man era. Trips often lasted a month or more, with pack strings of twenty-plus horses helping hunters to roam this vast mountain complex.

Many of Wyoming's most colorful characters were spawned during this period—tough, self-reliant fun-loving adventurers—literally "men to match our mountains."

Beginning with this story, I will attempt to chronicle some of these individuals in a collection called *Men to Match Our Mountains*. The first biographical sketch is about Ramul Dvarishkis, a ninety two year old cowboy, outfitter and horse breeder still living in Thermopolis.

It was fitting that I first met Ramul Dvarishkis in the Absaroka Mountains. I spent the night of August 31, 1979, camped near timberline in order to check bighorn sheep hunters when the season opened the next morning. Not long after first light, I heard a single rifle shot in the basin south of my camp.

When I finally located the hunters, I could see three handsome horses standing ground-tied at the bottom of the basin and several people with a bighorn ram. I remember being amazed that someone had horses so well trained that they trusted them to stand to a dropped rein in such a remote area.

Using an old bighorn sheep trail, I was able to reach the basin by traversing a long slope with thousands of rocks and boulders lying at an angle of repose. By then, the hunters had the ram packed on the horses and were moving down the trail. Ramul was in the lead, and he politely introduced himself and the hunter he was guiding.

Ramul at his hunting cabin at the edge of the Washakie Wilderness.
Photo courtesy of Jessie Dvarishkis.

In what I would later come to recognize as standard Dvarishkis hospitality, he invited me to dinner at his camp after I checked the sheep.

Looking back, it is amazing to think that Ramul was turning seventy that year. I would have guessed his age at no more than fifty. Ramul's business was a one-man outfitting operation. He packed everything in, set up camp and wrangled horses, guided hunters and cooked meals.

Several years later, I transferred to the Thermopolis game warden district, and had the good fortune to become friends with Ramul and learn more about his fascinating life.

Ramul was born in North Dakota in 1910, moving to Wyoming when he was seven years old. A natural hunter, he earned his first spending money trapping coyotes and bobcats near his parents' homestead on Cottonwood Creek. He used that money to buy his first Morgan stallion in 1928, and this began a lifelong passion for breeding and training Morgans.

While still a teen, Ramul broke and trained a big chestnut-colored Morgan named Discontent. Ramul was short in stature, so he trained the sixteen-hand horse to kneel so he could mount up. The horse would come on the run with a single whistle from Ramul, even in the biggest pastures. Rancher Paul Axtell was so impressed with the animal that he made Ramul an offer that he simply couldn't refuse. Stan Todorovich, one of Ramul's former wranglers, told me he never quite got over giving up Discontent.

During those early years, trips to Thermopolis for supplies were by horse and wagon and took up to three days. But Ramul loved those trips, as he was assigned to harness and care for the team of horses.

After his parents divorced, Ramul's mother married a sheep rancher named Arthur Hedgecock. From his teens until he was nearly thirty, Ramul spent each summer in the mountains herding and managing sheep. It was during these years that he obtained his intimate knowledge of the Absaroka wilderness. He also became fascinated by bighorn sheep, and he would later become one of the state's most renowned sheep outfitters. His last client was successful when Ramul was eighty-one. Ramul eventually built up his own cattle ranch that he operated until 1994.

During the decades Ramul ranched at the foot of the

The Dvarishkis Ranch on Cottonwood Creek
in Hot Springs County was Ramul's pride and joy.
Photo courtesy of Jessie Dvarishkis.

mountains, he continued to explore the wilderness. He built a hunting cabin in a strategic location and guided sheep and elk hunters in some of the wildest and most rugged country in the state, often packing twenty to thirty horses. Most clients were thrilled with their experiences, true adventures of their lifetimes.

Ramul continued to develop his strain of Morgan horse—sure-footed, smooth-gaited and with tremendous endurance. Many are beautifully colored, including blood bays, and a number have platinum-colored manes and tails. These horses were taken to shows around the state and won many awards.

When new game wardens or forest rangers moved into the area, they sought Ramul's advice on getting through the mountains. To this day, if you want to know the real lay of the land, how to get from one river drainage to another, which pass can be crossed safely, Ramul is your man. He once told me that he had spent many years sleeping on the ground in those hills—truly a life in the open.

Beyond being a great hunter and top hand with horses, Ramul is best known as a real gentleman. I have always been amazed at the courtesy he and his wife, Jessie, extend to everyone. If you stopped by their place, you'd better have time for lunch or at least coffee.

Hundreds of residents hunted on Ramul's ranch even though he had an outfitting business. Though happiest on horseback in the mountains, he did his civic duty, serving on school boards, working as a 4-H leader and attending sportsmen's meetings.

In this age of declining civility, highly competitive

hunting, locked gates and nasty dispositions in many quarters, we can look at Ramul Dvarishkis and see the way many of us should really want to be.

As a postscript, I called Thermopolis this morning to see how Ramul is doing at ninety-two. I found out that he had just had a horse wreck roping a calf. Imagine that.

Ramul Dvarishkis passed away March 2, 2004

Max Wilde skylines on his favorite hunting horse near Wapiti Ridge.
Photo courtesy of Buffalo Bill Historical Center, Cody, Wyoming;
Gift of the Barrus Family,
Marj, Mick, Jim and Page Barrus; P.301.1.11.

2

Max Wilde
A "Wild" Life for a Legend Named Wilde

No discussion of Wyoming's legendary hunters would be complete without a reference to Max Wilde—hunter, rancher and one of the state's most famous outfitters.

My interest in Max Wilde was sparked by priceless old hunting photographs shown to me by the late Jack Richard of Cody. Jack was the son of Fred Richard, who, along with Ned Frost, started one of the earliest ranching and hunting operations west of Cody. As a young game warden, I often stopped at Jack's photo studio to look at his fascinating collection of photographs and listen to stories about hunting trips that took place in the early days.

Cody rodeo creator Carl Downing, baseball legend Ty Cobb,
Max Wilde and baseball legend Tris Speaker stand with their trophies
after participating in a Max Wilde-guided big game hunt in the Thorofare.
Gift from Jack Richard, part of author's personal collection.

Upon retirement and the closing of his studio, Jack Richard invited game warden Dave Bragonier and me to review his collection and select six photographs each for reproduction. This was typical of the courtesy Jack extended to many people over the years.

One of the first photos I selected was the picture featured in this article: Max Wilde with Ty Cobb and other baseball greats as they finished a big hunt in the Thorofare country. I also selected another photo of Wilde with Mickey Cochrane, another baseball great, and these adventurous scenes prompted me to learn more about this famous hunter.

Max Wilde was born in Indiana before the end of the nineteenth century, and as a youngster he was fascinated by stories of trapping and hunting in the far north. In 1908, he made a trapping expedition to Canada, and a year later he moved up to Alaska to pursue his love of hunting and the wilderness. Like many of the rugged individualists of that era, he was off exploring on his own while still a teenager. This is hard to imagine in today's pampered society.

In 1913, Wilde stopped in Cody and, impressed with the country, went to work driving horse teams that pulled wagonloads of tourists through Yellowstone National Park.

As Wilde sampled the hunting and fishing in the Cody country, he knew he had found a home. Working for famous outfits like the Majo and Valley ranches, he also began packing hunters into the mountains.

In 1916, Wilde filed for a homestead on the South Fork of the Shoshone River, and he constructed a cabin to serve as headquarters for his hunting and trapping operation.

Pine marten and red fox pelts were extremely valuable

Max Wilde and "Phonograph" Jones coming out of the Thorofare
with their catch of furs from the winter of 1919-1920.
Photo courtesy of Buffalo Bill Historical Center, Cody, Wyoming;
Gift of the Barrus Family,
Marj, Mick, Jim and Page Barrus; P.301.1.5.

in those years, with marten hides fetching over twenty dollars each—a tidy sum in 1917. Wilde would run his trapline throughout the winter on foot, with horses or by skiing or using snowshoes—whatever the terrain and snow conditions dictated.

In 1918, Max Wilde met his future trapping partner, Ed "Phonograph" Jones. The two planned a major adventure: They would spend an entire winter in the Thorofare trapping. Establishing two base camps thirty miles apart, they placed caches of food and supplies in between.

Max Wilde with the catch of furs
that caused quite a stir in the Cody area.
Photo courtesy of Buffalo Bill Historical Center, Cody, Wyoming;
Gift of the Barrus Family,
Marj, Mick, Jim and Page Barrus; P.301.1.7.

Raw Furs. Displayed at The Cody Trading Co. Store, Cody, Wyo.
Fur Catch, Winter 1919-1920. Vicinity of Cody, Wyo. Value $10000.
Trappers, Max Wilde, E.L. Jones, Ed Holmquist. Victor Traps.
Fox, Marten, Coyote, Mink, Weasel, Squirrel. Electric Light Photo.

Max Wilde's and "Phonograph" Jones' furs were displayed
in the storefront of the Cody Trading Company
and word soon got around that they had received $10,000 for the lot.
As Max put it, "Everyone turned trapper after that."
Photo courtesy of Buffalo Bill Historical Center, Cody, Wyoming;
Gift of the Barrus Family,
Marj, Mick, Jim and Page Barrus; P.301.1.13.

Elk meat was the staple.

It is interesting to note that Wilde and Jones found the winter weather in the high country generally tolerable. I once interviewed another oldtimer, Del Beaver, later a guide for Max Wilde. Beaver spent a similar winter trapping marten in the high elevations of the Absaroka Range, and he said that many days were quite pleasant. As he told it, you could often take off your snowshoes and walk along the windblown ridges in your shirtsleeves. Del also described the technique used to store elk meat near timberline—wrapping the quarters in burlap and hanging them under a conifer bough.

Coming out of the wilderness that spring, Jones and Wilde had over 120 marten and a number of red fox. The furs were valued at over ten thousand dollars and were displayed in the storefront of the old Cody Trading Company. This catch caused quite a stir, as the value of those pelts far exceeded normal wages paid in those days. As Max put it, "Everyone turned trapper after that."

Renowned big game hunter Grancel Fitz with the "Grancel Fitz Elk,"
7 points on one side, 9 on the other,
with an inside spread of 64.25 inches Outfitter-Max Wilde.
*Photo courtesy of Buffalo Bill Historical Center, Cody, Wyoming;
Gift of the Barrus Family,
Marj, Mick, Jim and Page Barrus; P.301.1.60.*

Tom Yawkey, Boston Red Socks owner,
with a fabulous mule deer buck. Inscription reads,
"Best wishes to Max in memory of many happy Wyoming
hunting trips. Tom Yawkey."
*Photo courtesy of Buffalo Bill Historical Center, Cody,
Wyoming; Gift of the Barrus Family,
Marj, Mick, Jim and Page Barrus; P.301.1.35.*

Wilde trapped for several more years and used his savings to buy a string of packhorses. He began his career as an outfitter, basing his operation from the homestead, which by then was designated the Lazy Bar F Ranch.

Hunting trips in the early days usually lasted a month or more, and there were no restrictions on campsites or areas to be hunted. In addition, each hunter was entitled to hunt most big game species on a single license. The result was a large pack string roaming through the mountains with everyone hunting elk, deer, moose, black bear, grizzly bear and bighorn sheep with little or no competition. Great days, to say the least.

The reputation of Max Wilde spread quickly due to the quality of his operation and his personal abilities as a guide. Many baseball greats hunted with him, including baseball legends Ty Cobb and Tris Speaker.

One of the greatest trophies taken by Wilde's hunters was a famous elk shot by renowned big game hunter Grancel Fitz. Known as the Grancel Fitz elk, the rack had seven points on one side, nine on the other and was an incredible sixty-four-plus inches wide.

Other notable people guided by Wilde included Arthur Godfrey, Tom Yawkey, Bill and Dick DuPont and Bill Rae, editor of *Outdoor Life*. Many Wilde hunts were featured in the hunting publications of that time.

Wilde was an ardent conservationist and served on the Wyoming Game and Fish Commission in the late 1940s. A review of old commission records reveals several causes that Wilde championed, including better salaries for game wardens, a retirement system for Game and Fish employees, the creation of mobile check stations and the purchase of the Kerns Elk Winter Range Unit and the Ocean Lake Waterfowl Management Area.

Wilde retired in the 1960s, disliking short hunts and crowded outfitting conditions. If everything is relative to your past experience, one can see why change would have been hard for him to accept.

Even in his last years, Wilde remained thankful for the many wonderful outdoor experiences Wyoming provided him. He is remembered as one of the state's finest hunters and conservationists.

Ned was truly a "colorful character"
as depicted in this photo of him in a buffalo hide jacket
with his signature hat and a cub bear on his shoulder.
Photo courtesy of Buffalo Bill Historical Center, Cody, Wyoming;
Jack Richard Collection; P.89.2756.

3

Ned Frost
Inventing the Wilderness Hunt

Recent television documentaries have portrayed Daniel Boone and Davy Crockett as America's hunter heroes, and while I agree with that assessment, it should be remembered that in Wyoming we have a few of our own. First and foremost among them would be the late Ned Frost of Cody, who, along with Fred Richard, literally invented the concept of long-term horseback pack trips to hunt big game.

Near as I can tell, Ned was born around 1881 and was brought into the Cody country as an infant. His family wintered on the South Fork with a group of Crow Indians before establishing a ranch and roadhouse on Sage Creek near present-day Cody.

The first record of Ned's hunting prowess was when he shot a cattle-eating grizzly bear at the age of seven or eight. His father had asked him to check a bear trap on Sage Creek, and he luckily took along a Winchester .45-90 just in case. As he approached the site, a mad grizzly broke free from the trap and charged. Ned shot six times, hitting the bear five times in the chest. This would not be the last charging grizzly in Ned's life, and his amazing calm and accurate shooting became his hallmark.

Ned's son, Dick, wrote several stories about his father's adventures. Of particular interest is the tale of Ned's first meeting with Buffalo Bill Cody.

Ned and his father were taking freight wagons of game meat to Coulson, Montana, now known as Billings, and returning with supplies for the roadhouse. Ned was then fourteen and had been assigned to procure antelope for the next shipment. Just as he was about to shoot at a herd of antelope, a group of horsemen appeared. As the antelope spooked, Ned fired several shots, each killing an antelope cleanly. The leader of the mounted hunters turned out to be Buffalo Bill, and rather than being disappointed at having a youngster shoot game out from under him, he complimented Ned on his fine shooting and stalking.

When Ned Frost wrote about the early hunts in the 1890s, he described extremely abundant game in the Cody country. As he put it, "One never went over the high passes into the big country but would hunt around Carter Mountain, Greybull or up the North Fork, usually around the mouth of Elk Fork." He goes on to say that "in the earlier days, when you could ride out over the hills twenty miles south of here

Ned Frost (left) and Fred Richards
at their hunting camp in the Thorofare at the turn of the century.
Gift from Jack Richard, part of author's personal collection.

around the head of Sage Creek, Meeteetse Creek, Carter Creek
and a point of Carter Mountain, it wasn't unusual to see
five thousand antelope in a day's ride and perhaps two
thousand elk and deer thrown in for good measure." He also
reported bighorn sheep on the river bluffs where the town of
Cody now stands.

On these early rides, Ned began packing a small
camera, and he actually won awards for wildlife photography
as early as 1900. Luckily for us, this began a life-long interest
in photography that produced a wonderful historic record.

In the first years of the twentieth century, Ned "partnered up" with Fred Richard. Each took out adjoining homesteads on Green Creek, a tributary of the North Fork of the Shoshone River west of Cody. Fred married a woman from Chicago, and Ned then met and married her sister. They developed plans for a large ranch house, but funds were short.

As with many of the old-time hunters, Frost and Richard saw the lucrative fur market as a chance for a grubstake. Moving to an old log cabin near Clark, the pair set out three long trap lines, Fred taking on the role of skinner and stretcher, Ned using his natural hunting skills to hunt and trap. Coyote pelts were bringing up to sixty dollars apiece, a veritable fortune at that time.

By the spring of 1909, the two hunters had enough cash for the main ranch house, which they constructed prior to the September hunting season. The beautiful home had seventeen rooms, including a living room with fireplace and seven bedrooms upstairs, a perfect base camp for hunting the nearby wilderness.

Outfitting and guiding were virtually unknown at this time, but Fred and Ned saw great opportunities in the new tourist trade. Forming the Frost and Richard Company, they began hauling guests into Yellowstone National Park with horse-drawn wagons and white teepee tents under a large canvas banner bearing the Frost and Richard logo.

It was during one of these early expeditions that Ned had another grizzly bear encounter. It was an old male bear that had lost a toe in a trap and had also been previously shot and recovered from his wound. Having lost most fear of man, he was a dangerous character to say the least.

The handwritten caption on this old photo reads:
"Typical hunting trophies early this century—Thorofare,
Frost & Richard Outfitters."
Photo courtesy of Buffalo Bill Historical Center, Cody, Wyoming;
Jack Richard Collection; PN.89.17105.2.

The bear had attacked one of the outfit's top hands, Ed
"Phonograph" Jones, and Ned hit the bear with a stick of
firewood in an attempt to get the bear off of Jones. The grizzly
then attacked Ned. As Frost hid in his sleeping bag, the bear
grabbed him by the legs and started tossing him around. Ned
was able to grab a tree branch and pull himself up and away
from the bear, but he suffered several deep wounds.

Luckily, there was a surgeon from Vienna staying at the Yellowstone Lake Hotel, and he was able to patch the pair up by the light of the campfire. They were then transported to the ranch for recuperation.

At the same time, the two entrepreneurs began packing hunters into the wilderness. These were great adventures, often lasting thirty to forty-five days with pack strings of twenty or more horses. The photos you see here depict those days, and were given to me by Fred's grandson, the late Jack Richard.

After several years, Frost and Richard split up their business, each continuing in the outfitting industry in different capacities.

Ned Frost subsequently guided many notable figures on some classic hunts. One of the most famous expeditions occurred when Art Young and Saxton Pope—later namesakes of the venerable Pope and Young Club—enlisted Ned's help in securing grizzly bear specimens. They had obtained permission to hunt with longbow and arrow in Yellowstone Park, and the bears were to be placed in a museum.

Although many of today's archers know of the famous old male bear dubbed the "Dunraven Grizzly," which was taken by Pope and Young, few know of an earlier hunt that nearly ended in disaster.

Frost had located six or seven grizzlies resting in a snowfield on Mount Washburn. He maneuvered Pope and Young into position through a long stalk. At a distance of thirty yards or less, the archers let several arrows fly. One grizzly, hit by a metal broadhead, spotted the hunters and charged through the snow in great leaps. At point blank range,

Ned's old Model Ninety-Five barked and the bear fell dead between them. Once again, Ned was cool, calm and accurate in the face of danger.

Frost also guided Howard Hill, arguably the greatest American archer of all time. They hunted above Cody and Meeteetse for bighorn sheep, deer, moose and elk with Hollywood producer Jerry Fairbanks filming the entire hunt. Hill made several fantastic shots on game, and the film segment was dubbed *The Last Wilderness*. This short movie played in theaters across the nation for many years.

To illustrate the hunting ability and charisma of Ned Frost, one needs only to look at the influence he had on James Clark, author of *The Great Arc of the Wild Sheep*. His lifelong interest in sheep was sparked by a single hunt with Ned above Cody. Subsequently, he studied and hunted wild sheep around the world.

This short biographical sketch lacks the space needed to fully describe Ned Frost's life. He was truly a hunter's hunter, roaming the Wyoming wilderness for decades in search of game. His grizzly bear encounters alone would fill a small book. But perhaps the few anecdotes I have related will give the reader a glimpse of this adventurous and fine character.

Ned continued to hunt with his sons after the first wilderness trips were over, and he served as a mentor to many a young outdoorsman. Ned Frost's legacy lives on, and he will be remembered as one of Wyoming's true hunter heroes.

This ram was taken on Well's Creek in 1923.
Photo courtesy of Wyoming Wildlife *magazine.*

4

Ernie Faler
Wyoming's Greatest Sheep Hunter

One of the biggest mistakes young people in Wyoming can make is not taking time to visit with the long-time residents in their communities. Our post-frontier history is so close, you can almost reach out and touch it, and we still have old-timers around who knew the horseback era and worked with the colorful cowboys and hunters born in the nineteenth century.

I have always had an interest in the early days of Wyoming's hunting history and taken advantage of opportunities to meet many of the old hunters and trappers. And so it was when I happened to check an elderly angler on

Flaming Gorge in the 1970s, and seeing his pioneer license and 1893 date of birth, politely inquired about his background.

He turned out to be Ernie Faler, undoubtedly Wyoming's greatest sheep hunter, but initially I didn't make a connection with his name, which was well known to local residents.

Like many of the old-timers, he appreciated someone showing an interest in his life history and began to relate the fascinating tale of sixty years spent hunting in the mountains. When he told me he had taken sixty-two bighorn rams, I hurried back to my truck, grabbed my coffee thermos, a sandwich, returned and located a good flat rock to sit on while I listened and jotted down notes.

Luckily for me, the fish weren't biting, and after an hour or so of visiting, Ernie invited me to his home to view a collection of old hunting photographs. There were two old black photo albums brimming with fabulous pictures from the turn of the century. In addition to the numerous sheep hunts, he had photos of a twenty-one inch antelope he had taken near Pinedale and an incredible mule deer buck whose fifty-two inch wide antlers spread beyond the outside of an old touring car's hood. Sadly, he told me that the deer ended up in a bar in Alaska and was destroyed in a fire.

Ernie told me he was born in 1893 in the Hoback Basin. His parents had come west in a wagon train, and his father, Daniel, had opened Faler's Trading Post in the Hoback.

The fur trade was still quite strong in those days, and buying pelts was a significant part of the family business. Ernie said that some former cavalry soldiers stayed in that country to trap, and they hired him to skin for them.

A fascinating detail of this anecdote was the fact that he had skinned a large number of wolverines. When I queried him further on that point, he added that he and his brother, Arthur, caught over fifty wolverines as young trappers. This included one wolverine which had fought a mountain lion to a standstill, and the young hunters collected both animals.

It is interesting to note that wolverines became extremely rare during the subsequent decades of poisoning predators but are now showing signs of recovery. Another example of what can be learned from the old-timers.

Like most frontier families, the Falers had their share of tragedies. Ernie's father was shot and killed by an unknown assailant as he rode into his trading post, and his brother, Ralph, died in a snowstorm while delivering mail from Pinedale to South Pass.

Ernie shot his first ram in 1906 on the Greys River, and his sixty-second ram in 1962 in the Boulder Creek drainage.

In the early years, there were no seasons or bag limits, and Ernie once shot six rams with six shots near Black Fox Lake (the lake being named for a cross fox Ernie had caught there). Sheep and elk were the staple in their diet and, as Ernie once told an interviewer, "We hunted to live and we lived to hunt." Deer were very scarce at that time, and Ernie reported that he never saw a moose in the early days.

In the first years of big game regulations, you could still harvest two bighorn rams per year, and Ernie usually did. It was during this period that he became aware of a black, or *melanistic*, ram near Jackson. Pursuing the old ram for five years, Ernie finally caught up with him near Clyde Lake,

Ernie began his sheep hunting career in 1906.
In 1946, he returned from a hunt with these bighorns.
Photo courtesy of Wyoming Wildlife *magazine.*

which he named in honor of his son. It was a beautiful black ram, but he was extremely old, and Ernie said he probably would not have survived another winter.

In regard to hunting large predators, Ernie reported taking two grizzly bears, including a large male on the Roaring Fork. He also shot a wolf from a pack near Soda Lake while working as a cowboy. This, of course, was during the era of settlement, when the collective goal was to remove bears and wolves whenever possible.

Just as Ernie Faler witnessed the transition from the frontier era to modern big game management, he also progressed from a 45-70 black powder rifle to a bolt action 30-06. Most of his hunting was done with open sights.

Ernie later moved to Rock Springs, and he would take a four-horse team to the mountains for sheep and elk hunts. Another fascinating anecdote about that era is his report that some hunters used dogs to drive elk out of the forest. This is still a common practice in Scandinavian moose hunting (hence, the Norwegian elk hound), and it is probable that loggers and miners from Norway, Sweden and Finland brought that practice with them.

After nearly sixty years of hunting in the mountains, Ernie Faler's name became legendary. The Forest Service named Faler Lake after him and newspapers chronicled his hunts.

He continued the "easy hunts" such as antelope and prairie mule deer right up to the time I met him; however, you could tell his heart was still in the high country as he carefully told the story of each old photograph.

I returned to visit Ernie several times, often taking

another game warden, Randy Johnson, with me. He was always glad to see us and would break out the coffee mugs and photo albums. Our chance meeting was my good fortune, and it illustrates the value of taking some time to visit with old-timers who knew Wyoming before us.

David Prager always grew a beard and long hair during the winters.
His shaving was a sure sign of spring.
His first mountain lion was taken in 1953 after it killed one of his
colts, the first cougar taken in that country in fifty years.
Today mountain lions are abundant in that area.
Photo courtesy of Pat Mcateer.

5

David Prager
Latter-Day Mountain Man

It took something to stand out as an exceptional hunter or woodsman in the early part of the twentieth century. Nearly everyone in rural Wyoming hunted for a portion of their subsistence and trapped for extra income. But even in that era a few natural-born hunters stood out, and in the Laramie Range, that man was David Prager.

"Mountain Man" seems an apt description for David, as he was actually born in the mountains, spent his entire life hunting and ranching in that same mountain range, and, in the end, died working alone in a winter wilderness in his late seventies.

David came by his adventurous spirit honestly, with both sides of his family coming to Wyoming as pioneer ranchers. His grandfather, Frank Prager Sr., left the Estes Park area of Colorado in 1876, claiming it had become "too crowded." He settled in the Laramie Peak country not far from the location of today's Twin Pines Ranch.

A picture of Frank Prager Sr., in the 1870s is in the state museum, and it is a classic period photograph. Dressed in what appears to be a buckskin jacket, his hair is mid-length in the same fashion as Jim Bridger and Kit Carson.

Hostile bands of Sioux and Cheyenne Indians were still roaming the country when Frank Sr. arrived, and during one raid he hid in a beaver lodge while a war party burned down his cabin and haystack. Known to Indians as "The Laughing White Man," he would often smile and laugh during a confrontation with their warriors; this was totally disconcerting to them and led several tribes to believe he was charmed and protected by spirits.

The next generation of Pragers—Frank Jr., and his wife, Ellen—remained in the Laramie Mountains and built up a ranch. On April 15, 1911, Ellen gave birth to David at a place called Owen, Wyoming, near the present-day Hubbard's Cupboard.

As a very small child, David Prager's wanderlust and interest in nature were evident. His mother would place a turkey bell around his neck so she could monitor his activities near their wilderness home, and David would constantly request "My cap and bell, Mother," so he could be off on another small outing.

The site of the Prager family ranch was extremely

remote in the horseback era, and David attended a one-room country school. His teacher lived at their ranch.

David's teacher discovered that he was rising early to check his trapline before class, and felt that his grades would improve if he remained in bed and was more rested. In response, David began getting up in the dark, checking his traps at first light, and then jumping back into bed before the teacher awoke. Unaware of his new tactic, the teacher said she was quite pleased with his improvement in school, and credited the change to the fact that he was not "fooling with those traps anymore."

David's brother, Lawrence, who is still living in Douglas, was born in 1918. The two boys were destined to become lifelong ranching and hunting partners.

David contracted the 1918 flu during the worldwide epidemic that killed millions, and he consequently missed a year of school. He graduated from Wheatland High School in 1929. Always in top physical condition, he later took pride in the fact that he could wear the suit purchased for his graduation throughout his life.

Even as a young cowboy, David preferred walking to riding a horse. On their long cattle drives to the railhead at Medicine Bow, he could be seen leading his horse, mounting up only to rope or work a particular bunch of cattle. In an interview late in life, he was quoted as saying, "I got to walk to keep livin'," and, "When I'm out there walking in those hills, I feel free."

According to David's niece, Barbara Billingsley, her uncle was "rancher by occupation, but hunter by nature." Fixing fence or working cattle could always wait if he struck

David with a good antelope.
He preferred walking to riding a horse and always said,
"I got to walk to keep livin'."
Photo courtesy of Pat McAteer.

the track of a mountain lion or bull elk.

As elk populations were restored in the Laramie Range, limited hunting seasons were implemented. During the 1958 season, the two Prager brothers were looking for an elk when David encountered a monstrous old bull. Placing a shell in his gun, he somehow caught his thumb under the bolt and literally ripped it open trying to get it loose. By that time, the bull had run over the hill and was spotted by Lawrence. As Lawrence related the story, with a twinkle in his eye, he saw the bull rounding the end of a ridge—and running to the point above the bull, he fired, missing his first shot in the excitement and then "dropped him with my second shot."

The big bull scored nearly 390 Boone and Crockett points, and ranked twenty-first in the world at that time. Given David's fascination with hunting and trophy antlers, one can only imagine his chagrin over missing his chance at that fabulous elk.

One of my lifelong hunting partners, Pat McAteer, of Casper, became a good friend of David's over the years. Pat is a long-time official measurer for the Pope and Young Club, so he and David shared a common interest in horns and antlers. David had a large collection of both shed antlers and personal trophies—he would regale Pat with the story of each one. His voice would modulate as he told each tale, rising to an excited pitch as he reached the culmination of each hunt.

One great story was the time David had spotted a wild old mule deer buck with non-typical antlers, but was unable to get within range of him despite several careful stalks. Determined to harvest the big buck, he took his rifle, a bedroll and what food he could carry in his pockets and set out after his trophy. After four days of monitoring the big deer's feeding and bedding habits, he maneuvered close enough for a shot. I have seen the mount of that deer—it's a dandy.

David stayed in the mountains his entire life and rarely went to town. He heated his home with a woodstove, and never installed a water heater or flush toilet, instead heating water on the stove and maintaining an outhouse. His bedspread was a tanned deer or elk hide and he sewed buckskin onto the soles of his wool socks, so they could double as a moccasin when his boots were off. When he did get to town, he found the heated buildings intolerably hot and the beds too soft, often sleeping on the floor. Like the early mountain men, he became inured to cold weather. A great anecdote from niece Barbara was the time some fellow ranchers snowmobiled into the ranch to see how David was doing and placed their wet gloves on his stove to dry for the trip home. Getting ready to leave, they found their gloves frozen to the stove as it was not lit!

The one time David Prager would leave his home on Eagle Peak was to hunt wild sheep. He collected a grand slam of impressive rams from Arizona, Canada, Wyoming and Alaska. Departing for the far north, he would arrive at the Casper airport with his rifle and hunting kit, but instead of packing a suitcase, he would simply wear all of his hunting clothes in layers. He made quite a sight. They say that he found kindred spirits in the old Indian guides of Alaska and Canada.

During his hunt for a Wyoming bighorn, David was caught in a major blizzard and was missing from his camp for several days. A search was organized. When the storm finally broke, David emerged from his improvised snow cave with a trophy ram, furious to find out that folks were looking for him. His mother had been notified that he was missing, and simply dismissed everyone's concern, saying, "You don't have to worry about David, he will take care of himself." How right she was.

In later life, David continued to winter in the hills, and over the years became a master at catching coyotes by using the blind trail set. As he put it, "You just have to be smarter than the coyote."

When he was nearly seventy, David had a hip replaced, and during his first day back on the ranch, he climbed to the top of a haystack exclaiming, "Let's see if this hip's any good" and jumped off into the snow.

During late March 1988, David's neighbors had not heard from him by radio for quite some time. A nearby rancher went to check on him and discovered that his horse had not been fed and there was no sign of David. Organizing a search party, they discovered his body lying next to his snow machine. It appeared that he had gone out to retrieve some hay for his horse, and when returning, possibly in a blizzard, had driven off a cornice of snow into a pile of boulders.

In retrospect, his niece Barbara felt that he had "laid in state in his mountains" before his body was found. I was impressed by that thought.

If Wyoming had a latter-day mountain man, it was surely David Prager. His reputation as both a great hunter and true gentleman is solidly established in central Wyoming, and through this story I hope other folks will gain an appreciation of his interesting life.

Photo courtesy of Jean Dearinger.

6

Mel Stonehouse
Last of the Old Time Cowboy Hunters

Few pictures are truly worth a thousand words, but for me, the 1938 portrait photo of Mel Stonehouse really has it—evoking the golden years of rodeo in Wyoming and the West. At first glance, the handsome face and classic Western attire of that era strike you as belonging to some star of the silver screen, but upon closer examination you notice the rough calloused fingers which could only belong to a real cowboy.

This picture, along with a championship saddle and other rodeo gear, rested in a glass case in the Cody Holiday Inn nearly thirty yeas ago. I was working at that time with the late George "Sonny" Reesey, a long-time game warden and native of the Big Horn Basin, and we passed the display on our way to lunch one day. Sonny told me Mel had been a colorful cowboy and rodeo star who later guided and outfitted near Pahaska Tepee. Sonny guided for Mel as a young man, and he related several great stories about their early adventures hunting big game in the Cody country.

When I began writing this series, I was determined to learn more about the man in that portrait. I contacted an old friend and former game warden, Randy Johnson of Laramie, who had also guided for Mel. Randy put me in touch with Jean Dearinger, whose father had virtually raised Mel, and she directed me to Mel's wife and children in Cody. Following several interviews, I began to piece together the life of this fascinating cowboy and hunter.

They say tough beginnings create tough people—and this could never have been more true than in the case of Mel Stonehouse. Born near Oak Creek, Colorado, in 1912, where his parents ran a small ranch, he would be only two years old when his first hardship began.

The spring storm of 1914 dropped thirty inches of snow in twelve hours, and caught his parents and their team of horses halfway to Steamboat Springs. Leaving the wagon, they tried to make it on foot to the nearest ranch. Two days later, their frozen bodies were found huddled together in a shallow ravine.

Initially, Mel and his brother and sister were placed in the custody of an uncle, but within weeks he had put them up for adoption. Placed in an orphanage near Denver, Mel led a hard life for a three year old, with meager rations, difficult chores and potential beatings being the order of the day.

When only seven, he was taken to a farm and began

working in the fields. At age nine, he was fed up with poor treatment and, grabbing his .22 rifle and a few clothes, took off on foot. He had heard of a fellow named Vandergrift who ran the horse and mule livery in Denver, and seeking him out, was fortunate to find the first person who would show him a little compassion.

A natural with horses, he was introduced to I.B. Humphrey, a trainer who took thoroughbreds to races in Tijuana, Mexico. At the ripe old age of ten, Humphrey sent Mel to Mexico as a jockey.

A veterinarian named Doc Dunlevy looked after him at the racetracks, and Mel described him as "a dandy old man—one of my first real friends." In an attempt at generosity, Doc outfitted him in knickers and long stockings, but Mel was ridiculed by the other jockeys, and having learned to defend himself in the orphanage, would end up in a fight every time. He finally convinced Doc to quit buying him those "silly socks."

At about that time, Mel was introduced to stock operator C.B. Irwin, who is best known as the owner of the famous bucking horse, "Steamboat," inspiration for Wyoming's official logo. Irwin took Mel from Tijuana to Toronto horse racing but Mel was gaining weight as he obtained some decent nourishment and became too heavy to ride as a jockey. An admirer of Mel's horsemanship, Irwin sent him to his Cheyenne ranch to break horses and punch cows.

Mel's natural talent with horses was augmented by sage advice from old-time cowboys like George Mullins. He was soon breaking broncs with the best of them.

His first rodeo experience occurred at Medicine Bow,

then a major stockyard and shipping point. Sixty cowboys threw in ten bucks each, and they then created an arena by circling cars and wagons. As Mel later told his son, Rick, "I'll be damned if I didn't draw a heck of a horse, and I won the whole damn thing, six hundred dollars."

It would be several years before he won again, but he had the fever for sure. Rodeo became more organized in the

Mel rides high in the air on "Black Gasher" during a winning ride at the 1933 Cheyenne Frontier Days rodeo.
Photo courtesy of Irene Stonehouse.

1930s and Mel was in the thick of it. At sixteen, he rode in Cheyenne and was introduced to Ed McCarty, who owned McCarty and Elliot, a big rodeo stock outfit at that time.

During a subsequent rodeo, one of McCarty's bucking horses, Broken Box, kicked Mel in the head and, being unconscious for days, Ed decided to haul him to his ranch near Chugwater after he got out of the hospital. According to Ed's daughter, Jean Dearinger, her dad literally adopted Mel, and it was the first family experience of his life.

Mel became Ed's "try-on" rider and "test rode" thousands of horses over the next decade. Newspaper clippings of that era refer to Mel and the McCartys as the "Chugwater Cowboys."

In that era Ed McCarty owned both "Midnight" and "Five Minutes to Midnight," and according to Mel, "I rode Five, but there wasn't enough rope in the state of Wyoming to tie me on ol' Midnight." In fact, he was never "rode"—despite several false claims.

As a carryover from the old Wild West shows, Ed McCarty sent Mel and other cowboys to Madison Square Garden, London and Sydney, Australia to put on a big show.

When they reached Australia, there were no horses ready for them, so they went to the outback, caught some brombies (wild horses), and broke them well enough in three weeks to rope and bulldog off them.

Coming home from Australia on the steamship *Mariposa*, there was a big dance one night. Mel was dancing with this "good lookin' old gal," who turned out to be a prostitute. When Mel figured it out, he made some offhand remark and, becoming incensed, she wanted her pimp to fight him. Mel was glad to oblige.

A big cowboy offered to referee, and they went up on the top deck. In the typical fashion of his trade, this big old pimp was dressed to the nines and decided to remove his dinner jacket before the fight started. He took it off and was looking for a place to put it, when Mel said, "Here I'll hang it up for you." The pimp handed it to Mel, who promptly threw it overboard. Turns out it contained his passport, money and stateroom key, and the man just sat down and "went to crying." There was never any fight.

During the heyday of his rodeo career, Mel spent several winters in Hollywood doubling for famous cowboy actors. His good looks and horsemanship were always in demand. He knew Tim McCoy and became friends with Ben Johnson and Richard Farnsworth.

Mel rode in the Cody Rodeo in 1940, and immediately took a liking to the country. Recuperating there after a bull broke his ankle, he met his future wife, Irene, "The best lookin' gal in the state of Wyoming." They were married two years later.

In the 1940s Mel worked on the J-9 Ranch west of Cody, and began a family. His oldest son, John, and daughter, Kathy, were born there. He continued to rodeo occasionally and, in 1945, was the only cowboy to ever ride the bucking horse, "Walter Winchell."

When the J-9 sold, Mel began trapping beaver for the Wyoming Game and Fish Department. A natural hunter all his life, he "caught too many beaver, and trapped myself out of a job."

Henry Coe, owner of the famous resort, Pahaska

Mel Stonehouse (left) shows off a bear hide following a successful hunt with well-known trapper and hunter Roy Glasgow.
Photo courtesy of Irene Stonehouse.

Tepee, near Yellowstone's East gate, soon offered Mel a job running his "horse outfit," a dude ranch operation which included outfitting big game hunters.

Out of rodeo for the most part, he happened to be at the Cody arena in 1950. They were short of bronc riders. Asked to ride, he was bucked into the fence by the horse "Owl Creek," which belonged to stock contractor Merle Fales. He suffered a compound fracture of both his tibia and fibula, and this harrowing injury put him in the hospital for more than a month.

Told to rest and recuperate at home—Mel just couldn't stay still for long. Two guides, George "Sonny" Reesey, and Merle Fales, were about to take some elk hunters into the high country, and Mel figured he had to be along. Riding with his cast propped forward, they ran into a big storm on the Thorofare plateau. His cast began softening.

According to Merle Fales, by the time they got to the hunting camp, Mel's cast was "the shape of his horse's side." Merle and Sonny went to a nearby cabin, where they found a small apple barrel, some bailing wire and Plaster of Paris left by Max Wilde on an earlier hunt.

Placing the barrel staves on the outside of the cast, they fastened them with bailing wire and poured plaster over the whole thing. The end result was a cast the diameter of a small tree trunk.

When they finally got out of the hills, Mel was taken to a doctor. They forgot to explain the components of the improvised cast and as the doc' began cutting through it with a small electric saw, he hit the wire and sparks began to fly!

The leg never healed properly. Mel eventually developed osteomyelitis and often had an open wound to contend with. He rode and packed with that bad leg through thirty years of pain, often tossing a jug of whiskey into his saddlebag just to help him get down the trail.

With his natural hunting ability and genuine cowboy persona, Mel developed a successful hunting business. Among his most famous clients were General Jimmy Doolittle and Roy Rogers, both of whom became personal friends. As Mel put it, "The general and Roy were great guys...they weren't any different than anybody else, they still put their pants on one leg at a time."

One of Mel's hunting camps was Buffalo Bill's historic Camp Monaco and early photos show the famous tree carved with the Camp Monaco inscription next to his tent.

Mel's camps were in the heart of grizzly bear country, and he would often have a bear visit his camp. On one trip, he heard some commotion around midnight and, looking out of his tent, saw a big old grizzly taking a bucket of hot chocolate off the cook stove. Mel grabbed a section of stovepipe and swatted the bear on the butt to get him out of there. The bucket slid over the bear's head and he took off into the trees. As Mel related to son Rick years later, "He must've run into a

Game warden "Shorty" Meyer (left) and Mel relax in hunting camp. Two of Mel's guides, George "Sonny" Reesey and Randy Johnson, later became Wyoming game wardens.
Photo courtesy of Irene Stonehouse.

tree or something, because pretty soon I hear him coming back toward camp, and I'll tell you he's on the fight."

Game Warden Earl Thomas was in camp that night, and he helped Mel build a roaring fire to keep the bear at bay. The grizzly circled their camp the entire night.

After hunting professionally for twenty years, Mel decided he didn't want to deal with the new age of Forest Service regulations and restrictions placed on commercial operators. He moved downstream to operate Sweetwater Lodge as a dude ranch.

Meeting up with some old cowboy friends—the Curtis Brothers—who ran the Two Dot Ranch and Cody Night Rodeo, Mel reverted to his early life: cowboying in the winter and acting as rodeo arena director in the summer.

By 1981, Mel had endured more than thirty years of pain with his leg, and a doctor friend advised, "Mel, why don't we just cut the damn thing off," which they did.

Incredibly, Mel returned to ranch work as soon as the amputation healed, confirming what his youngest son, Rick, has written about him—he was "tougher than a boot."

In his last years, Mel was painted by several artists, including the famous western portrait painter James Bama.

Mel Stonehouse passed away in 1989, and thus ended one of the most colorful lives of 20th century Wyoming.

Many thanks to Mel's wife, Irene, his son Rick, granddaughter Yancy Blankenship, Jean Dearinger and Randy Johnson for their help in putting this story together.

Leonard "Curly" Corbin prepares to enter a hewing contest
at the Woodchoppers Jamboree when he was in his mid-60s.
Photo courtesy of Bruce Corbin.

7

Leonard "Curly" Corbin
Wyoming's Hunting Lumberjack

Many of my most poignant memories of early childhood center around the times spent with my grandmother when she operated the Elk Mountain Hotel and its famous dance hall in the early 1950s. Long before the interstate came through, it was a wild and remote place with a charm all its own for someone interested in the outdoors.

The majority of my grandmother's lodgers were lumberjacks who worked in the Snowy Range. As the saying goes, they were men "as hard as their axe handles," but many of them would befriend me as a young boy. At my least sign of boredom, they would produce a razor-sharp pocketknife and whittle out a perfect wooden sword or a beautiful whistle; I wish I had kept one. And I can vividly remember one big fellow who helped me rig up an old metal fishing pole so I could catch a big brown trout I had spotted in a pool out behind the hotel. Great days.

One of the most interesting lumberjacks who lived in Elk Mountain in that era was Leonard "Curly" Corbin, an old-time tie hack and renowned hunter. Nearly fifty years later I would interview Curly at the age of ninety-eight and learn about his adventures in the mountains of Wyoming.

A good friend, Wade Fraley, who works at the Veterans Administration Hospital in Cheyenne, was arranging a talk I was to give at their nursing home when he happened to mention a World War I veteran who had spent his entire life in the mountains hunting, trapping and working as a logger. I asked Wade to arrange a visit, and I packed along my tape recorder and notepad.

Leonard Corbin was born on August 22, 1901, in Afton, Iowa, the son of Lory and "Homewood" Corbin. His parents owned a small farm, but he had no interest in becoming a farmer.

At the age of sixteen, Leonard lied about his age and enlisted to fight in World War I, serving as a crew chief on the early bi-planes. Several years after his discharge, he rejoined the army and was sent to the Philippines. From there, he was sent on a cruise of the Orient and told me that he walked on the Great Wall of China while still a teenager.

Out of the army for a second time, Leonard decided to head west, arriving at a lumber camp in West Yellowstone, Montana, in 1923. He learned to cut railroad ties with a broad axe, hewing trees he cut on the flat where the town of West Yellowstone stands today.

Leonard was extremely skilled with his razor-sharp axe, and became a marketable commodity. During the 1920s, he cut timber in one form or another in Montana, Idaho, Wyoming, Colorado and New Mexico.

Leonard grew his hair to a mid-length in the fashion of the old mountain men, and between his hair length and natural curls, was dubbed "Curly," a moniker that would stick for life.

Curly's first love was hunting, and the remote timber camps gave him access to the wilderness, at that time the last refuge of big game which had literally been extirpated at lower elevations. Early photos show a proud Curly with various mature bull elk, rare prizes in that era. Although he occasionally packed horses, he would usually walk into the high country and pack game animals out with a pack frame. One can only imagine the physical condition he was in.

Curly told me that he loved living in the mountains and, when possible, subsisted on wild game. He kept two cast iron skillets; one for game, one for fish.

Wanting to stay in the hills, Curly would work as a tie hack in the summer and fall, and then travel to Utah's canyon country or New Mexico and hunt predators for the big stock outfits of that time. He became an expert at catching depredating mountain lions, and this trade allowed him to winter in the milder climates of the southern Rockies. His descriptions of that period made it sound like heaven for an outdoorsman.

Like many of the old hunters I have known, Curly's

Harvesting a mature bull elk in the 1930s was a rare feat.
Photo courtesy of Bruce Corbin.

anecdotes involving wildlife were extremely accurate and descriptive. A good example is his story about the last wild wolf on the Laramie plains. It was an old white wolf that always stayed out of rifle range, and Curly said he could remember seeing it on the prairie near Centennial "standing there with his long legs on the short grass – he looked like a Shetland pony."

In 1928, Curly began working in the Snowy Range, and participated in eight major railroad tie drives. Each drive involved 250,000-300,000 ties, and they moved them downstream from the head of Douglas Creek to the railroad at Fort Steele.

Tie hacking was incredibly dangerous, as evidenced by two of Curly's tales:

One time down in Brush Creek we had a center (the build-up of ties) down in the middle. I went down on ahead to open the channel a little...In this center was a rock about seven to eight feet high. Behind it was a little platform, just below water. So, when I pulled that center, I decided I'd stay there and fend them ties off the rock to keep that channel open because it was pretty narrow in there if you didn't keep that one open. Well, I was just doing fine and then the rear boats turned loose a center above me that had several thousand ties in it. When they hit that rock, they went plumb over my head in a sheet. I was lucky, I had deep water behind the rock. I dove down just as deep as I could and I stayed underwater as long as I could. Finally, when I got up, I was in between centers there and those ties were just rolling past. I didn't dare get a couple between my knees, or I'd lose my legs. So I just spread my pike pole out between my

*(outstretched) hands, spread my legs and rode those tumblin'
ties on down the river until they thinned-out and I could get
out on the bank. I thought I was dead that time, but I wasn't
even hurt. I started back working and pretty soon the rest of
them come around the bend. And, to show how they'd kid
you in them days, they said, "By gosh, it didn't kill the damn
fool after all!"*

And...

*Once we got the ties to the North Platte, a few of us
would ride in the water with the ties. I was a wing and
center man and they wouldn't let many men do that. It took
me a couple of years before they let me do it. You'd grab a
couple of floating railroad ties between your knees and take
your pike pole and go down the river, just like in a kayak. In
the white water, like Brush Creek Canyon, all of them rocks
in there would hang the ties and they'd build up for many
hundreds of feet, sometimes floating, sometimes not. What
I'd do, and I was really the only one allowed to do it steady,
was to paddle down the river and hit the head of the center.
When you hit it, you'd have to roll right up on top of the pile,
or else you'd get sucked under the water.*

Throughout this period, Curly continued big game
hunting, and developed an interest in trophy animals. He told
me that he shot nearly fifty mule deer bucks in the thirty inch
class, including a monstrous nontypical with over thirty
points which he killed at the head of Horse Creek near Dubois
and then packed out on his back.

Curly (left) and his logging partner, Frank Sterns,
pose with their hunting trophies
in the interior of their tie hack cabin near Dubois in the 1930's.
Photo courtesy of Bruce Corbin.

During the 1930s, Wyoming had many game preserves closed to hunting, but as big game recovered they were opened to the limited harvest of buck deer and bull elk. One of the largest, the Teton Game Preserve, was opened in the late part of the decade, and Curly headed into the wilderness for an elk hunt. The bull he shot was so large that a tourist in Jackson Hole offered him a hundred dollars for it—this being at the end of the Depression.

Curly joined the army once again during World War II, and thus became a "retread," a description applied to veterans of both world wars. After the war, Curly returned to his lumberjack life, first near Dubois and later he moved to Elk Mountain.

Sometimes a single incident will reveal an individual's hunting prowess; a good example being this story from my uncle, R.V. Bailey. R.V. was staying at the Elk Mountain Hotel in 1955 when they opened one of the first elk seasons following the restoration of local herds. Curly was to guide some fellow to a big bull he had spotted, but told my uncle to position himself in a grove of trees above them and a young bull should come by on a nearby trail. Not long after first light, my uncle heard a shot down below and, just as Curly had predicted, a young bull soon came along and R.V. harvested one of his first elk.

Throughout the 1950s and 1960s, Curly continued logging, often winning local hewing contests where the other contestants were half his age.

The bachelor life was Curly's only option since he stayed in the hills for decades, but when I asked him about women, he just winked and told me not to worry, he usually "knew a girl or two in most of the towns."

In his later years, Curly moved to Rawlins, where he became very active in veterans' affairs. He served as Wyoming Department Commander of the Veterans of World War I and eventually became National Commander in 1993, at the age of ninety-two.

When I visited with Curly at the age of ninety-eight, he was still in good physical shape and his mental acuity was sharper than many men at sixty. He was then subscribing to seventeen publications; reading them all cover-to-cover. Terry Cleveland, our assistant division chief, received Christmas cards from Curly up until his death, and said his penmanship was a beautiful cursive, including the final card.

Curly took this photo of a trophy class moose eating his horse hay.
Note the perfectly cut and stacked kindling alongside the cabin.
Photo courtesy of Bruce Corbin.

Leonard "Curly" Corbin passed away on Sept. 16, 2000, among his fellow veterans at the Cheyenne V.A. Hospital.

A common theme with the old hunters who spent their life in the mountains of Wyoming is a value system which places our state's intrinsic qualities near the top; its mountains, wilderness and wildlife are the memories they hold most dear. Curly was no exception.

What will our memories of Wyoming be? Of shining mountains and sparkling streams, or of shopping malls and fancy houses. Time will tell.

Sam Young, Jr. on his famous hunting horse, "Steel." His traplines and hunting territory involved some of the most rugged terrain in North America. This big gelding had a smooth and fast gait combined with the stamina necessary for the mountains.
Photo courtesy of Judy Toland.

8

Sam Young Jr.
Legendary Hunter of the Greys River

Most of the legendary hunters and trappers featured in these stories were either known to me personally or I had heard of them through old hunters and game wardens over the years. As the series progressed, one of my goals became writing about a renowned hunter from each of the major mountain ranges.

This past fall I was hunting for a good mule deer buck in the high country of the Greys River drainage when it dawned on me that I didn't have a candidate from the Wyoming Range. Surely there was some fascinating character from such great game country. There was no doubt in my mind about who to contact for ideas, as Afton game warden Duane Hyde has worked in that drainage for thirty-one years and is a native of Star Valley.

Duane had been following my hunting stories and knew the type of individual I was looking for. Without hesitation he recommended Sam Young Jr., an old-time hunter and trapper who lived year-round on the Greys River for more than fifty years. He was also good enough to put me in contact with Sam's daughter, Judy Toland, a gracious lady who was more than willing to help me put this story together.

Sam Young Jr. was born on Aug. 5, 1913 in San Francisco to Sam and Helen Young. Sam Sr. was a career Army man, and young Sam spent his boyhood on Army bases, first in California and later at Fort Russell near Cheyenne.

While stationed at Fort Russell, Sam Sr. was put in charge of the Pole Mountain Military Reserve. Helen was an ardent hunter, and this duty station allowed her to pursue that interest. An early Cheyenne newspaper clipping credits her with killing a large gray wolf that had been raising hell with local livestock.

The family left Cheyenne in 1926, after Sam Sr. had been caught making moonshine for the third time. They traveled first to Montpelier, Idaho, then the family eventually ended up in the Greys River Valley on June 8, 1927. While they were camped out that first night, they heard a strange thundering noise to the northeast. Days later they found out that the Gros Ventre dam had broken, washing out the town of Kelly. The noise had been a torrent of water rumbling down Snake River Canyon.

Sam and Helen, along with their two young boys,

Sam Jr. and Rex, built a log cabin on White Creek, at that time the farthest point you could reach by road. Their building materials were secured from the nearby forest and the cabin was built in the same fashion as those constructed by the early mountain men.

Although they had a few staples like flour and beans, the family was down to less than two dollars in cash and would have to rely on a rifle and several gunnysacks full of traps to make a living and put meat on the table.

As fall arrived and furbearing animals became "prime," old Sam and the boys began trapping beaver, marten, mink, otter and coyotes. They made a good catch and, along with money they made the next summer cowboying, were able to purchase a team, wagon, saddle horses, and other supplies. In addition, the boys' mother, Helen, would occasionally shoot a deer, elk, or moose for the larder.

The Young family got their original grubstake through trapping. Money received for furs was their only cash flow in the early years. *Photo courtesy of Ila Young.*

Life in the wilderness was hard, but it suited the Youngs. They made ten-foot skis from pine and fashioned snowshoes from serviceberry limbs and buckskin thongs. As Sam Jr. would later recall, there were two seasons on the Greys: "July and August, and winter."

There were only two pieces of private property in the drainage. Both were homesteads, and the family eventually owned them. The upper piece, obtained from Jim Moffat, was later developed into the famous Box Y Ranch by Sam Jr. and his wife.

Two coal mines began operating in the Greys River, the Vail and Blind Bull mines. The family opened a small store and truck stop complete with a lunch counter for the truckers. Sam Sr. went to Afton looking for a waitress and recruited Ila Thorton, who was working in a local cafe. When she met young Sam, it must have been love at first sight, for within six weeks Sam Jr. and Ila were married on Nov. 15, 1937.

Not long after their marriage, the Vail mine exploded. Unaware of the tragedy, Rex Young was woken by a barking dog. He got dressed and went out in the sub-zero weather where he recognized a little dog he had seen at the mine. He followed the dog up Deadman Creek toward the mine, and soon discovered Carrie Baker, whose son and husband were two of the five miners working through the winter. Dressed in no more than a housedress and slippers, she had tried to make it out on skis to report the accident. Injured and frostbitten, she was close to death.

Rex took Carrie to Sam and Ila's cabin, and the two brothers headed back into the dark, frozen night on skis with a toboggan full of blankets. They followed the woman's tracks on the six-mile trail to the mine. They could see where she would ski only a short distance before falling down due to inexperience and the fact that the skis were built to fit a large man. When they reached Vail mine they found it was totally destroyed and there were no survivors. The mine never reopened.

At about that time Sam Jr. was employed as a government hunter, a post he would hold for thirteen years. Coyotes were the emphasis of his control work, as the region was fully stocked with domestic sheep at that time. Trapping the high country of the Wyoming and Salt River ranges meant negotiating some of the toughest terrain in North America, and although he owned many horses, Sam's favorite hunting horse was "Steel," a big blue roan that could really cover the ground.

His coyote trapping required making a big circuit—often being gone for four or five days, sleeping on the ground or staying in line shacks and improvised cabins. Sam also continued to run his own winter trapline, and was hunting in one form or another year-round. Some winters he would catch close to one hundred marten—worth a considerable sum in those days.

Once each winter he would make a trip for supplies, traveling on skis or snowshoes with a pack frame and toboggan. He had his choice of two arduous routes: Either fourteen miles up and over the Salt River Range, or thirty miles down the Greys to the cabin of Joe Gillis, another trapper and fascinating character of the time. These trips are almost unimaginable today, and reflect the level of fitness and elan possessed by men like Sam.

On one winter trek for supplies, Sam was caught unaware by a big avalanche along the Greys. He was swept away by the cascading snow and knocked unconscious. But he finally came to when the impromptu snow dam created by the avalanche backed up the river into him. He crawled to a nearby empty ranger station and laid there in recuperation for ten days.

The Greys River valley had phone service for a period of time during the 1940s, and Sam received an emergency phone message on March 2, 1945. The Forest Service district ranger reported that a plane conducting elk surveys in the Greys was missing, and that a snow coach and search party would pick him up in the morning. The Forest Service felt that Sam was the only person fit and tough enough to snowshoe up over Middle Ridge and scout for the missing plane.

When the rescue party was delayed, Sam headed down-country on his snowshoes to begin his own search. When he got to Moose Flat, approximately five miles downstream, he found a snowshoe sticking up in the road. He fired his pistol in the air and heard someone call out down near the river. Upon investigation, he found game warden Bob Brown lying under a big spruce tree.

Bob was in tough shape, with broken ribs, a smashed and frozen hand, injured back, broken jaw, and missing teeth. He was able to tell Sam that the plane had crashed at the head of Moose Creek, killing pilot Dick Johnson and Forest Service biologist Orange A. Olsen. Bob had managed to start a fire with his last two matches, and stayed at the crash site overnight. When he slipped into unconsciousness, he awoke to find himself covered with more than a foot of new snow. Since the plane could no longer be seen from the air because of the snow, he figured his only chance was to head towards the Greys. Using the plane's life-saving snowshoes, including one for a crutch, he eventually made it to the river where he was found by Sam.

Sam placed Bob on a bed of spruce boughs, started a fire on either side of him, stacked up extra kindling, and then ran on his snowshoes back to Deadman Ranch—covering the distance in forty-five minutes.

Airplanes were used to ferry guests to the Boy Y Ranch
in both summer and winter. Many of the planes were built
at the CALLAIR factory in Afton, Wyoming,
including this beautiful old plane built in the 1940s
Photo courtesy of Judy Toland.

Sam called in the emergency and found out that the search party couldn't get a snow coach to run. So he took a bottle of whiskey, a thermos full of chicken broth, and a toboggan with blankets and headed back down, accompanied by his mother. After feeding Bob some broth despite his mouth being "torn to hell," they rolled him onto the toboggan and returned to the ranch.

The search party did not arrive until 1 a.m. and there was no doubt in anybody's mind, including Bob Brown's, that Sam Young saved his life.

Airplanes were allowed to land in the Greys during the 1940s and 1950s, and great period photos of that era show guests arriving at the Box Y by plane, including winter photos with planes on skis and folks deplaning in topcoats and dress clothes. Many of these beautiful old planes and their skis were manufactured locally by CALLAIR of Afton, and Sam Young, along with brother Rex, used these planes to conduct winter snow surveys at elevations up to 10,000 feet.

During the 1940s, Sam, Jr. and Ila purchased the Box Y from old Sam and began building a guest ranch. They built a lodge with seven cabins and Sam constructed the majority of the furniture from lodgepole pine he cut in the forest. It was masterful work, and the chairs, sofas and tables are still in use today.

Sam, Ila and their three daughters accommodated summer guests with fishing and wilderness horseback rides, and Sam developed a successful big game outfitting business. His specialty was bull elk and trophy mule deer—no one knew the high country like he did. His years of riding and trapping had shown him where the old bucks and bulls hung out, and

Sam Young, Jr. seated back right, relaxes with
hunting clients in the old lodge at the Boy Y Ranch.
He built all the furniture
from Lodgepole pine he cut in the nearby forest.
Photo courtesy of Ila Young.

his reputation spread far and wide.

Sam's love of fishing never abated, and there are many pictures of him standing in the Greys with trophy class cutthroat trout. His daughter, Judy, told me that the best cutthroat he ever caught exceeded in length the width of their picnic table—a big fish, to say the least.

Sam sold the Box Y in 1970, and built a summer home nearby. He continued to hunt and trap the Greys River until just before his death in 1992. At the age of seventy, he could still walk through the willow bottoms carrying two fifty-pound beaver and a pack full of traps.

Understanding the lives of great hunters who went before us can enhance our appreciation of Wyoming just as surely as knowledge of history in other forms. Their legacy is not one of development or empire building, but rather a heritage of hard work and adventures beyond our wildest dreams; often leaving the country as they found it—wild and untrammeled.

I went up the Greys recently, and as always was struck by the towering peaks and verdant valleys. It doesn't look much different than when Sam got there in 1927, and my new understanding of his life history made me appreciate the country just that much more.

A Camp in the Forest
This wonderful old photograph shows Albert Nelson
on patrol as Wyoming's first game warden.
From the J.E. Stimson Collection,
Wyoming State Archives,
Department of State Parks and Cultural Resources.

9

Albert Nelson
Hunter, Outdoorsman, and
Our First Game Warden

For those who study the history of wildlife conservation in Wyoming, the bleakest period in terms of declining game species is the era from 1870 to the end of the nineteenth century. Opportunities to preserve dwindling populations were lost at every turn; market hunting and indiscriminate shooting by settlers occurred in a free-for-all atmosphere. The last remnants of many elk herds in the smaller mountain ranges and foothills were wiped out; migratory traditions among many bighorn sheep herds were lost with the elimination of sub-populations; and, despite protests in certain quarters, the last group of twenty-five to thirty wild bison in the Red Desert of southwestern Wyoming were shot in 1889.

It was during this time of exploitation that immigrant Albert Nelson arrived in Wyoming. Born and raised in Sweden, he had served in the Army and studied at an agricultural college where he worked extensively with horses. As a boy, he was fascinated by a Swedish translation of James Fenimore Cooper's *The Leather Stocking Tales*, and longed to see the American wilderness. After taking passage on a German freighter, he landed in New York in 1883. He then rode an empty freight car to Nebraska, was discovered and kicked off the train, worked in the hayfields a short time, then hopped another train to Rock Springs, arriving just weeks short of his twenty-fourth birthday.

Albert's knowledge of horses served him well in the wild West, and he soon found work as a cowboy. His granddaughter, Dena Nelson-Stilson, allowed me to copy an 1889 portrait of Albert in those early years. He is decked out in full cowboy regalia, including embroidery on the flared cuff of his gloves and a Colt .45 on his hip.

Much of the range was still open in those first years, and Albert roamed from Brown's Hole to South Pass. He became an accomplished hunter and crack shot, with many a chuckwagon cook relying on him to keep their outfit supplied with fresh game meat.

At some point in the late 1880s, Albert partnered up with an older fellow named Billy Bierer. The two of them hunted, trapped, and prospected along the Wind River

Albert Nelson, circa 1889,
working as an open-range cowboy
in southwestern Wyoming.
This was the same year the last wild bison
in the Red Desert were shot.
Photo courtesy of Dena Nelson-Stilson.

Mountains, and decided to homestead on the East Fork of Green River in 1888. Luckily, they laid in a supply of game meat and staples, for the ensuing winter was horrific, killing the majority of livestock and big game in much of the state. Since they had shared their supplies with neighbors, Albert and Billie soon depleted their own stores and were forced to snowshoe seventy miles to Rock Springs, returning with heavily laden toboggans.

Albert became a consummate outdoorsman, and sought out every opportunity to make his living in the open. He began guiding hunters and taught himself taxidermy; he was soon quite proficient, and hunters began bringing him their trophies for mounting.

In the fall of 1894, Albert and Billie trapped in the Jackson Hole country, building a small cabin on Flat Creek. They had success hunting and trapping and since they liked the country, they decided to homestead.

In early July 1895, a posse appeared at their cabin to enlist them in an effort to apprehend Indians from Idaho who were killing elk for their hides. Albert offered to go along on his first of many experiences related to wildlife protection. After apprehending the Indians on the upper Green River, the posse seized 211 hides. Several Indians were taken to Evanston for trial, but were later released due to vagueness about jurisdiction and the unclear language of early game laws.

Albert filed for a homestead on the Gros Ventre River and began building a home there. He resumed his big game guiding and taxidermy work, and his reputation for quality hunting trips and trophy mounts soon brought him some fascinating customers.

The Harrimans and John D. Rockefeller, Jr. were among his clients, as was the famous author Ernest Thompson Seton. Seton was so impressed with his taxidermy specimens that he tried to persuade him to relocate with a big firm of New York taxidermists. Albert declined.

Noted artist and photographer, J.E. Stimson, took numerous pack trips with Albert in search of wilderness subject matter. He also taught Albert photography and film development. His photograph of Albert titled, *A Camp in the Forest*, now hangs in the Wyoming State Museum.

Another interesting client was the painter Carl Rungius. The two men became fast friends, and Rungius took every opportunity to ride the high country with Albert. On one trip, Rungius broke his leg near the head of the Green River. Albert packed the artist as far as South Park and a doctor was summoned from Jackson. Arriving with whiskey on his breath, the doc set the leg and applied a cast in a hurried fashion. When he departed, Rungius asked the other hunters if they thought his leg had been set straight and none of them felt it had.

Albert cut off the cast and ground it up; then the other men pulled the broken leg and separated the break so he could reset the bones. They then dissolved the plaster of Paris and Nelson used it to apply a new cast.

The leg healed perfectly, and several months later a packing tube arrived in the mail along with a letter from Rungius. Thinking it was a calendar, Albert forgot to even take it from the post office. On his next trip, the post mistress reminded him it was still there, and when he opened the package it contained an original painting of a bull elk. Albert's granddaughter, Dena, showed me the picture, and it is a fine example of Carl Rungius's big game illustrations.

At the age of thirty-nine, Albert met Sarah Avila Allen, who had come to Jackson's Hole in 1896 with her parents. Here was a woman after his own heart—she loved to hunt, ride, and dance; they were soon married.

In 1899, Albert Nelson was appointed the first state game warden by Governor DeForest Richards. His appointment was endorsed by many notable citizens and sportsmen of the state.

Sarah Avila Nelson, Albert's wife.
They both loved to ride, hunt, and dance.
When she died at the age of thirty-four, Albert was heartbroken; never having interest in another woman.
Photo courtesy of Dena Nelson-Stilson.

Early day Wyoming lawmen in classic formal attire of that period.
Wyoming's first two state game wardens, Dan Nowlin (left)
and Albert Nelson are seated in front.
Both had been open range cowboys of the frontier era.
*Photo courtesy of Wyoming State Archives, Department of State
Parks and Cultural Resources.*

Yet Wyoming's new game laws were generally held in contempt by those holding on to frontier traditions. Albert made numerous arrests and rode horseback to trials across the state, including several in Cheyenne. But the courts turned a blind eye to the continued slaughter of dwindling big game and Albert was unable to obtain a single conviction for wildlife crime. After three frustrating years, he resigned.

Albert Nelson in his taxidermy shop in the town of Kelly.
This building was destroyed by the Gros Ventre flood of 1927.
Photo courtesy of Dena Nelson-Stilson.

Adversity often brought out the best in Albert; an illuminating example is the time when his young daughter, Anna, was injured in a fire. The local doctor told them there was little to be done, but Albert sterilized one of his razor-sharp taxidermy knives and carefully cut away infected skin and proud flesh. It was a horrific task for a parent, but his daughter lived through the ordeal and had minimal scarring. Anna, at ninety-four, still lives in Jackson, and I doubt that you could find anyone who has more reverence for a father.

After giving birth to seven children, Avila passed away on December 4, 1913; she was only thirty-four years old. This changed Albert's life in a dramatic way. Since he was determined to keep his children together, he sold his ranch and moved to Kelly. He opened a taxidermy shop, and between making a living and caring for seven children, had time for little else.

He was obviously heart-broken after losing his wife and best friend and would never have interest in another woman. His daughter, Anna, told me that he was still a handsome fellow and loved to go to the dances in Jackson; but he had lost the love of his life and had no desire for romance.

Albert's troubles continued when, in the spring of 1927, the natural dam which had formed Lower Slide Lake on the Gros Ventre River gave way and washed out the town of Kelly. The flood claimed six lives and destroyed every business, including Albert's taxidermy shop.

After relocating to Jackson, Albert worked until his mid-eighties—at that time being the oldest practicing taxidermist in America. He carved many beautiful ornaments from horn and antler, including a pair of tall lamps with spiraling branches and leaves along their bases, each perfectly carved from thin sections of antler.

Fortunately, Albert lived to see wildlife protection become a reality and game herds recover throughout the state. He was able to teach his children and grandchildren how to hunt, fish and get along in the woods. He remained active until his death at the grand old age of ninety-five.

After visiting with old-timers who knew Albert Nelson, there is one common denominator: They all say he was a tremendous outdoorsman and a man of sterling character. That is a legacy to take pride in.

This incredibly detailed portrait of Anson Eddy
was painted by Wyoming artist James Bama.
Bama knew Eddy well and reports
"Anson seldom went anywhere without a rifle
—for he might spot a rabbit which would provide his supper."
Artwork courtesy of James Bama.

10

Anson Eddy
A Life in the Wilderness

If there is one outstanding characteristic of the old-time hunters and trappers that roamed Wyoming's backcountry, it is the love of solitude and an ability to survive on their own in a wilderness setting. Exemplifying that trait was Anson Eddy, who spent nearly sixty years living alone in a simple log cabin in the Absaroka Mountains.

Anson's early life history is somewhat obscure, but according to his own account, he was born in 1893 in an Indian wigwam in Vermont. His mother was a member of the Mohawk tribe; his father was a "renegade white man."

At the age of eight or nine, Anson was sent to a

relative's ranch near Sweetgrass, Montana. From there he moved to Canada as a teenager, arriving just in time to join the Canadian Army and ship out for combat in World War I. Returning home, he then served time with the Royal Canadian Mounted Police.

While serving as a Mounty, Anson met and married an Indian woman. Following a period of infatuation, the pair found they "didn't get along," and Anson left both the marriage and Canada.

Heading south to the Yellowstone country, Anson found work constructing and maintaining trails and telegraph lines for the Park Service and Forest Service. He was immediately enamored with the wilderness of Wyoming, and his innate love for animals led him to excel at handling horses. According to his long-time friend, Floyd Rathbun, Anson always walked and led a packhorse, claiming horses were to "carry his burden—he would carry himself."

In 1926, Anson Eddy filed for a homestead on Ishawooa Creek, a tributary of the South Fork of the Shoshone River west of Cody. To "prove-up" his homestead he dug a crude irrigation ditch; but he was no farmer, and the newly named Horse Head Ranch would serve as a base for hunting and trapping expeditions into the surrounding wilderness.

In addition to building a cabin on his homestead property, Anson went up to the high country and constructed simple trapline cabins to serve as shelter during the winter when marten pelts were "prime." There are still six to eight foot high stumps near timberline where Anson cut firewood during winters when snow depths were that high on level ground.

With no obligations down below, Anson would spend

months trapping pine marten in the mature forests of the Absaroka Range. Concerned that he would deplete marten populations, he devised sets that would attract more males than females. As the winter wore on, coyotes would begin utilizing his well-packed snowshoe trail, often stealing marten from his traps. He would then bait the trails as he went along—pushing small meat scraps into the snow. Then, prior to wrapping up his marten trapping, he would capture the conditioned coyotes whose pelts approached marten in value.

Anson trapped on through the 1930s and was reported to have raised an orphan calf moose which he would ride with a halter to retrieve his mail during periods of deep snow. Although he was a teller of tall tales—it appears that one was true.

When World War II broke out, Anson went back into the service, shipping out for Burma in 1942. He was assigned to pack mules through the jungle in support of Merril's Marauders. It was in the jungles of Burma that Anson met Wyoming native Floyd Rathbun; the two would later reunite in the mountains of Wyoming and spend years hunting together.

Following the war, Anson returned to his mountain cabin and resumed his trapping activities. He also earned extra money guiding hunters for such notable outfitters as Max Wilde and Ned Frost. Among his clients was outdoor writer Jack O'Connor. Known for his intimate knowledge of the country and ability to find game animals, he was featured in several hunting magazines, including *Outdoor Life*.

It was during the early 1950s that Anson was injured

Anson Eddy built high country trapline cabins
to serve as shelter as he snowshoed and trapped pine marten.
Photo courtesy of Steve Ronne.

The same cabin nearly forty years later.
A forest fire has passed just behind this historic old structure.
Photo courtesy of Steve Ronne.

Anson Eddy with some high-country coyotes.
Trapping was his primary source of income during his entire life.
Photo courtesy of Greg Dodson.

by a young bear. The bear was caught by the toes in one of his coyote traps, and he decided to release it unharmed. Stories conflict over whether it was a black bear or grizzly; but regardless, it failed to appreciate Anson's good intentions, and as it was released from the trap attacked him—injuring his thigh and lower leg. He limped back to his cabin to recover. Floyd Ruthbun said the eventual scarring was extensive.

Living with his horses and handling them on a daily basis, Anson was able to achieve levels of training seldom seen today. He had crossed Morgans with draft horses to create a stout pack animal, and Floyd Rathbun recalls a time when they would send those horses out of the high country loaded with elk quarters with a simple slap on the rump. The horses would return to the cabin where Gene Patton of Cody would unload the elk and feed the horses. He would then put the pack saddles back on and send the horses back up the trail; the highly conditioned animals traveling many miles back up to Anson's hunting camp. Pretty amazing.

During the 1960s, Floyd and Anson came upon two orphaned mountain lion kittens about six miles up the trail from the cabin. Anson took them to his cabin and began providing big game meat for them. They stayed around the cabin for over a year; resting with ease around Anson and yet dashing for cover if another human approached. Reaching adulthood, they finally moved off on their own.

Anson also loved cats and often had twenty or more living with him. He dug a small hole under the foundation to serve as a cat door—and when the occasional skunk entered the cabin, he would calmly wait for it to leave—the animals never sprayed him.

In the fall of 1970, Anson Eddy was arrested and charged with first-degree murder. Noted western artist Bob Meyers had been shot and killed while fixing fence on his ranch below Anson's homestead. He and Anson had evidently been feuding over the use of the access road to Anson's place, as it went through Meyers yard. Although Anson never owned a vehicle and refused to drive, he did have friends bringing him supplies, and that was the point of contention.

Meyers had been killed by a bullet which had passed

through several fence posts and provided little to no forensic evidence. Anson had many rifles, but the prosecution could not make a ballistic match with any of them. In addition, his earlier admission of guilt was recanted; Anson claiming that he had signed a statement to simply "get the thing out in the open."

The trial generated national publicity and was featured in detective magazines of that era. Many notables testified, including both Alan and Milward Simpson. Among the character witnesses for Anson were many old-time cowboys and hunters who knew him well.

The jury of nine women and three men returned a verdict of not guilty in the case, and Anson was set free. The judge later admitted he was stunned when Eddy came in carrying his cowboy hat—a sure sign he felt he would be found innocent.

Anson returned to his mountain cabin and resumed his wilderness life. In 1975, his cabin burned—destroying his belongings. Among the lost memorabilia were several gold Spanish coins he claimed to have found in the high country of the Absaroka range. He had never revealed the exact location of that find, as he didn't want people "ruining the country."

Friends brought him a trailer to live in, but it was also lost in a fire; possibly the result of Anson's careless cook stove techniques. Determined to provide him with shelter, Anson's friends then built him a cabin of cinderblocks with a dirt floor—about as fireproof as you could get.

Anson roamed the wilderness even in his later years; out-walking men half his age. For his eightieth birthday, he decided to hike up Yellow Creek to the top of Wapiti Ridge—

Anson Eddy spent decades living alone in this wilderness cabin.
Photo courtesy of James Bama.

he did it with impunity.

Anson Eddy was found dead at the age of eighty-eight. He was lying next to a bucket of water he was retrieving from Ishawooa Creek, having apparently had a heart attack.

Anson had chosen a wilderness gravesite a few minutes walk from his cabin. From there, you could see the sun rise and set—and the site commanded a view of the beautiful Ishawooa valley. Over one hundred friends attended his memorial service.

Dressed in wool from head to toe
and carrying a rifle slung over her shoulder, Mary Price
remained in my memory as the consummate mountain woman.
Photo courtesy of Mary Myers.

11

Mary Price
A Woman to Match
Both Men and Mountains

First impressions can be indelible, and such was the case when I first met Mary Price. The year was 1967, and I was visiting with Sonny Price at his Mountain View Ranch in the Buffalo Valley of Jackson Hole. We were discussing mule deer hunting and other important matters when a lone rider appeared on the slope we were facing. Sonny told me it was his mother and that I should meet her, as she was one of the best hunters in that country.

Even before Mary dismounted, her countenance told you she was on the fight. Turns out she had just caught some fellow hunting off a bear bait she had placed in the Lava Creek drainage and where she was planning to guide a hunter. She related to us that she had warned the hunter not to return if he valued his personal safety and there was no doubt in my mind that she meant every word.

Dressed in wool from head to toe and carrying a rifle slung over her shoulder, Mary Price remains in my memory as the consummate mountain woman.

When I began writing this series, the notable Wyoming hunters and trappers that came to mind were all male, hence the title: *Men to Match Our Mountains*. But as the series progressed, I recalled my encounter with Mary Price and knew she should be included.

I contacted my old friend Lewis Ray, who is a longtime Casper taxidermist and had introduced me to Sonny Price. Lewis had worked in Jackson Hole when he first arrived in Wyoming, and the Price family had befriended him, showing the newcomer the wildest places in Jackson Hole and how to get along in the wilderness.

Lewis directed me to Mary's daughter, Mary Myers, who still resides in Jackson. Mary and I had several good visits and she also loaned me some great old family photographs of her mother.

Mary Price was born Mary Barbara Wolff on May 6, 1911, at Elk, Wyoming in Jackson Hole. Her parents, Emile and Marie Wolff, were pioneer settlers in the Jackson country with Marie being credited as one of "Jackson Hole's first white women."

Emile Wolff had immigrated from Belgium and, along with a Robert Miller, had homesteaded the present townsite of Jackson. He later returned to Belgium to care for his sick mother, and there he met and married Marie in 1893. When they returned to Wyoming, the couple homesteaded in the Buffalo Valley; digging an irrigation ditch by hand to bring water from Spread Creek, nearly five miles away. Marie's prize possession was a piano, and it was packed in over Teton Pass.

Grizzly bears were an ever-present hazard in the early years, and Emile became one of the region's most proficient bear hunters. Not long after they constructed their homestead cabin, a young trapper friend was mauled by a grizzly. His face had been torn open and his tongue exposed, his left ribs were laid bare and his left arm nearly severed at the shoulder. Emile sewed him back together with string from a gunnysack, and he was cared for by Marie until he recovered.

Mary and her two brothers, Willie and Stippy Wolff, helped with the homestead chores, but they were also taught to hunt and trap in order to keep the family supplied with meat and to procure furs to trade for groceries and supplies. Each spring the family's catch of fur was taken to Idaho Falls and exchanged for a wagonload of supplies. Mary and Willie were both natural hunters and crack shots; their hunting and trapping "chores" being a labor of keen personal interest.

Mary attended school at Elk for six years, but was soon back working at the family ranch. While an early teen, she began guiding hunters, and was known for her riding and shooting abilities.

At the age of nineteen, Mary met and married Lewis Price, and the couple moved to Moran, where her husband worked at Jackson Lake dam. After several years, they moved to the "Wallace Place," a ranch property near Spread Creek, and while Mary worked the ranch, Lewis continued working at the dam.

Mary and Lewis would eventually have seven children, Donna, Judy "Pat," Margie, Elmer, Lewis Jr. "Sonny," Marion "Winks," and Mary "Babe." As time went on, Lewis became less dependable as a provider—he had a penchant for saloons and the bright lights of town. Most of the responsibility for raising the family fell to Mary.

Mary poses with a bighorn sheep trophy
and her trusted .25/35 Winchester saddle gun.
She carried this rifle slung over her shoulder with a leather thong,
and with it, she harvested every major big game species in Wyoming.
Photo courtesy of Mary Myers.

When her mother passed away, the National Park Service purchased the original family homestead for Grand Teton National Park. Mary took her share of the proceeds and purchased the Buffalo Valley Ranch, a small place strategically located for hunting and trapping operations. With seven children to support, she began guiding hunters in the fall and trapped all winter. Any remaining time was devoted to raising her kids.

Mary guided elk, moose, sheep, and deer hunters—but her favorite pursuit was bear hunting, both black and grizzly. Perhaps this had been passed on from her bear hunting father.

Her trapping operation included marten, mink, otter, coyote, muskrat, and the occasional lynx or wolverine. Her outdoor talents were often summed up with, "She can out-hunt and out-trap any man I know."

Mary's trademarks during the 1950s and 1960s were her hunting horse, Goldie, and her Winchester .25/35 saddle gun. She always carried the rifle slung with an old leather thong as she rode her favorite mare through the hills.

A diminutive cartridge by today's standards, the .25/35 pushed a 117-grain bullet out of the barrel at around 2,200 feet per second. But with her stalking ability and expert marksmanship, Mary took every major big game species with the little saddle gun, including countless elk.

To get an idea of the Goldie's stamina, you simply have to examine Mary's marten trapping technique. As the snow would begin to deepen and marten pelts became valuable, she would begin breaking a trail up into the mature forest habitats, often riding the old mare each day along her trapline in order to keep the trail open. Tough horse, tough woman.

Mary Price poses with a catch of coyotes.
Note the marten, mink and otter pelts hung over her saddle.
This was Mary's favorite hunting horse, Goldie,
who carried her through the mountains for decades,
finally lying down behind the ranch to die at the age of thirty-four.
Photo courtesy of Mary Myers.

Once Mary was riding Goldie with her daughter, Mary, riding behind the saddle, when a cow elk broke over the ridge. In a split second Mary raised the old Winchester and fired, dropping the elk in its tracks. A hunter soon appeared and attempted to lay claim to the elk. Mary levered in another shell and rode forward, informing the man that the elk had been shot by her and that she had seven kids to feed. She gave him a chance to retreat before he had a "broke leg." The hunter quickly retreated.

Mary depended on Goldie for decades; the two covering thousands of miles in the wilderness. At the age of thirty-four, the old mare went out behind Mary's house, laid down and died.

In addition to guiding hunters and trapping, Mary found other ways to wrest a living from the wilderness. She grew a mountain garden and stored her home-canned vegetables and game meat in a deep cold spring. She caught washtubs full of whitefish and smoked them for later eating. In the late summer, she would hang empty pails over Goldie's packsaddle and lead her children on expeditions to gather chokecherries and wild strawberries.

The black bear mount was Mary's pride and joy.
At the time she shot the bear, it was considered to be one
of the biggest specimens ever to come out of the Jackson Hole area.
Photo courtesy of Mary Myers.

Mary's children learned to help their mom, often coming home from school to find an elk to be skinned or a frozen coyote to be fleshed and stretched before supper. Everyone chipped in as they led their rugged, yet rewarding, life in the mountains.

As Mary entered her seventies, her mental acuity diminished, foretelling the early symptoms of Alzheimer's disease. Although her thought processes were no longer clear, it was still evident that her mind was focused on the wilderness. Sonny would find her wandering the banks of the Buffalo in the middle of the night, beaver traps in hand.

When she was finally hospitalized, her mind remained occupied with a lifetime of adventures; cautioning a nurse about a bear in her room or, as Mary Myers described it, "huntin' and fishin' her way down the hospital hallways."

Mary Price passed away on December 10, 1988. Perhaps her obituary in the *Jackson Hole News* said it all "She spent her life guiding hunters, and in her free time enjoyed hunting, trapping and fishing on her own."

Kenny releases a beaver as part of an effort
to restore populations eliminated during the fur trade.
George Grunkemeyer photo
courtesy of Wyoming Game and Fish Department.

12

Kenny Martin
The Cowboy Game Warden

Prior to the second world war, Wyoming maintained a relatively small game warden force. Big game herds were still recovering from near extirpation at the end of the 19th century, and limited license sales kept revenues and department staffing at a minimum.

Early game wardens patrolled immense districts, and the relative lack of roads required the use of horses on a regular basis. It is not surprising that many of these old-time wardens had spent their early years as cowboys and ranch hands. They were often hired as game wardens in the county where they had grown up; their intimate knowledge of the country and backcountry skills being the best credentials in those days. Kenny Martin is a case in point.

Kenny was born in 1909 on his parents' homestead in the southern Absaroka Mountains of Hot Springs County. At the earliest age, he was taught to ride and shoot. His parents expected him to herd cattle and provide game meat for the table. Thus began his lifelong interest in horses and hunting.

In the early years, both money and game were scarce, and Kenny told me how he was expected to procure both small and big game with economy; one .22 shell should produce a rabbit, one .30-30 shell a deer or elk.

Kenny's family was known for innovation when it came to making a living from the land. While in their early teens, Kenny and his sister, Marion, would head for the badlands with their father and uncles to capture wild horses. When greenbroke, Kenny and Marion would drive the horses up Owl Creek and cross the Owl Creek Mountains at Blondie

Kenny and his sister, Molly, observe the sale
of wild horses they had trailed to Jackson Hole in 1928.
On the first such trail drive, they were twelve and thirteen years of age.
Photo courtesy of Mike Martin.

Pass. From there they would drive their herd up the Wind River Valley, over Togwotee Pass, and down into Jackson Hole where they sold the horses to dude ranches. Prior to the horse sale, the two teenagers would comb out the horses' manes and tails, not only improving their appearance, but also providing enough horsehair to trade for a new saddle.

The Martin family often packed their horses and went on big hunting or fishing expeditions. On one outing to the Bull Lake country, Kenny's grandfather, J.M. Cover, was bitten by a tick, contracted tick fever, and died before they could get him packed out of the hills.

Kenny's father, E.W. Martin, taught him how to manage a cattle herd, and he soon filed on his own homestead in the Copper Mountain area. During the early 1930s, he partnered at times with Paul Axtell of Thermopolis, who had a neighboring homestead.

Kenny (left) and family
with a nice catch of trout from Jackson Lake in 1930.
Photo courtesy of Mike Martin.

In 1938, the Wyoming Legislature passed into law a requirement that all game warden appointments be based upon competitive examinations. Their goal was to eliminate political favors and nepotism from the selection process, and the first exam was held in Casper in 1939. Kenny was a strong advocate of wildlife protection and management, so he traveled to Casper to take the exam. Scoring near the top, and endorsed by local sportsmen, he was appointed the game warden in Hot Springs County on March 1, 1939. At that time, there were twenty-four game wardens covering the entire state

Among Kenny's early duties were the trapping and transplanting of beaver, elk and bighorn sheep to areas where they had been eliminated. Wyoming's beaver restoration program was far and away the largest in the nation, and

Kenny with a fabulous bull elk
he took near his homestead on Copper Mountain in 1938.
Photo courtesy of Mike Martin.

Kenny, with his dashing good looks, was often featured in photos promoting the effort.

When World War II broke out, Kenny decided to enlist at the age of thirty-three. His life in the outdoors as a cowboy and game warden served him well in the Army. He set rifle marksmanship records at Camp Perry that stood for decades and was assigned as a first scout for the infantry in Europe; subsequently being decorated for his front-line reconnaissance during the Battle of the Bulge. The German infantry surely met more than their match in Kenny Martin.

Upon his discharge, Kenny returned to the Wyoming Game and Fish Department and was assigned to the supervisor position in Sheridan. He held that post for nearly twelve years before taking the supervisor position in Jackson. When he left Sheridan, the local sportsman club presented him with a Winchester Model 70 rifle in his favorite

Kenny with a pair of good antelope in 1940.
He had just gone to work as a Wyoming game warden.
Photo courtesy of Mike Martin.

Game wardens Kenny Martin (left) and Bob Frizin
operating a check station near Sheridan just after World War II.
Photo courtesy of Mike Martin.

caliber, .30-06. The engraved inscription on the floor plate commended him "for a job well done."

Kenny was stationed in Jackson for twenty years, and he was perfectly suited to the task. His hallmark was a cowboy hat cocked slightly to one side and a pair of leather gloves with his "Rocking K" brand on them in the right rear pocket of his jeans. Duane Hyde, retired game warden and classic.Western figure in his own right, told me that when he first met Kenny, he reminded him of one of the handsome silver screen cowboys from the early Westerns.

Fair, honest and hardworking, Kenny soon created his own celebrity in Jackson Hole. He could interact with folks from every walk of life, and his reputation preceded him wherever he went.

Kenny Martin (right) stands atop the elk burial ground
in the Lamar Valley in 1962.
Park rangers were shooting the elk to reduce populations,
and Kenny was an arch critic of their actions.
Photo courtesy of Wyoming Game and Fish Department.

The Jackson area allowed Kenny to pursue his interest in hunting and fishing. He and his wife "Gene" (short for Genevieve) soon had their children along and every family outing included a .22 rifle and several boxes of shells. By the time they were old enough to hunt, his children were crack shots.

Kenny's daughter, Laurie, is an ardent hunter and angler to this day, and she provided several poignant stories of

Kenny was commonly seen on horseback,
whether checking cows or hunters.
Photo courtesy of Mike Martin.

Kenny with a bighorn ram in 1935.
Still wearing his chaps, he was never in the hills
without a good saddle horse.
Photo courtesy of Mike Martin.

her childhood and outdoor adventures with her father.

"I can remember fishing in the evening from the shore of Jackson Lake with my dad when I was about four years old. Dad's lure of choice was a red and white daredevil. I was so small that I could only wade out about three feet into the water before it got too deep, so Dad would hold me and wade out and let me cast over his shoulder.

"Dad had to actually sneak out of the house to leave me at home, so I guess it was just easier to take me along! My job on the hunting trips up the Gros Ventre was to hold the horses when we got into the elk, since I was too young to hunt. Sometimes we still had horses when the smoke cleared, and sometimes we didn't, but we always had an elk and a few pretty long hikes!"

Kenny Martin and game warden Sonny Reesey
relax in the forest at Two Ocean Pass.
Photo courtesy of Wyoming Game and Fish Department.

Kenny's son, Mike, recalled his father's legendary marksmanship and told me, "I don't know that I ever saw him miss in my life."

In 1974, Kenny retired and returned to Thermopolis with his wife, Gene. They purchased a modest home in town, and Kenny immediately returned to his cowboy life. It was during this second cowboy career that I first met Kenny. I was stationed as a game warden in Thermopolis at the time—the same position Kenny had held in 1939.

You had to earn Kenny's respect, and my opportunity to do so came unexpectedly. Game warden Tim Britt and I were investigating a reported elk poaching on Copper Mountain when we apprehended two fellows rustling cattle; roping and shooting cows, then hauling them off in an enclosed camper. Kenny had felt there were too many missing cattle from some of the bigger outfits on the mountain, and the arrest confirmed his suspicions. He waved me down on a dirt road and said simply, "Well kid, I heard you and Britt caught those rustlers." From then on I was in good stead with Kenny Martin.

And in another situation, Kenny found me with a cracked transfer case on the opening day of elk season. He immediately insisted that I take either his ranch pickup or his favorite saddle horse to continue my patrolling. Another game warden, Jim Oudin, showed up on the scene to pick me up, but that generous offer was pure Kenny Martin.

Kenny passed away in 1995 at the age of eighty-five. His death was mourned by ranchers, cowboys, wildlife managers and sportsmen from across the country.

Photo courtesy of Wyoming Game and Fish Department.

13

John Aeschbach
Guardian of Little Horn Canyon

Given the modern abundance of elk, it is easy to forget that most Wyoming elk herds had to be reintroduced following the frontier period of market hunting and unregulated shooting by settlers. One of the first transplants involved the trapping of elk in Jackson Hole during the winter of 1909. The elk were then hauled by sleigh over Teton Pass, placed in railroad cars at St. Anthony, Idaho, and transported to Sheridan. Incredibly, most of the animals survived. After being held in the Sheridan City Park for recuperation, they were taken by horse and wagon to the foot of the Bighorn Mountains and released.

Having experienced the loss of elk in the Bighorns and then putting forth these Herculean efforts to reintroduce them, the citizens of Wyoming were adamant that the re-established herds be protected and allowed to rebuild. Although there were many dedicated game wardens who played a role in early elk protection efforts, John Aeschbach stands out among them.

John Aeschbach was born on March 14, 1897, apparently in upstate New York. Particular aspects of his family and childhood are virtually unknown; the only facts being that around the age of fourteen he decided to head west, against the wishes of his family.

John's aspiration was to become a cowboy, and he soon hired on with the old Tschirgi Cattle Company, which had a big spread on the north end of the Big Horn Mountains. There was still some open range in that era and John lived the old-time cowboy life—sleeping on the ground, eating at the chuckwagon and learning to ride and rope from cowboys who came into the country with the last cattle drives.

Carrying a pistol and rifle was standard practice at the time, and John soon demonstrated proficiency with both weapons. He could fire a Colt pistol proficiently with either hand—a talent admired and valued by early cowboys.

Feuds between sheep and cattle operators persisted in the early 20th century, particularly in the Big Horn Mountains. John related to retired warden Max Long that one of his early cowboy duties was keeping sheep and their owners off the cattle ranges.

John interacted constantly with the neighboring Crow Indians, even hunting with them at times. They taught him to hunt and he came to understand their dialect and how to "sign."

In the late 1920s, John homesteaded a small ranch in the remote Little Bighorn Canyon country, known locally as the "Little Horn." He ran a few cows, trapped and guided a few hunters to make a living.

At some point he met his future wife, Anna, a Swedish immigrant. She soon adapted to mountain living; learning to shoot and ride with great proficiency. Their day began around 4 a.m., with a pot of black coffee and a slice of fresh apple pie every day of the year.

John took great interest in the fledgling elk herd, and in 1939 traveled to Casper to take the first game warden examination. After passing the test, he worked occasionally as a temporary employee until he was hired permanently in 1953. Given that his cabin was situated in some of the best elk habitat in the country and the department had a desire to protect elk, they stationed him at that remote location.

John's patrols were almost entirely on horseback, and he established thirteen caches of supplies in trees and caves so that if necessary, he could stay in the field for weeks at a time. His only rations on patrol were a saddlebag full of homemade jerky, coffee, and a pot to boil water. He slept in the open to avoid packing tents, and had numerous caves and improvised shelters to utilize if a storm rolled in. He called these places "homers" and said that when he got down in one of them he always "perked up a little." At his cabin, he slept on an animal skin spread on the floor.

For John Aeschbach, the only way to protect elk was to basically live with them. He would camp within view of a

John Aeschbach's cabin on the West Fork of the Little Bighorn River.
He spent decades working as a game warden from this location;
often being gone on horseback for weeks at a time.
Photo courtesy of Wyoming Game and Fish Department.

large herd, and several would-be poachers were apprehended when John tapped them on the shoulder as they were stalking one of "his herds."

Typical of many good horse trainers, John's handling technique combined firmness and consistency with compassion. Al Badgett of Sheridan recounts how John once took a two year old stud he was training on its first trip into the mountains. John was leading the horse and each time he would stop the horse would keep walking and step on his heels. Al asked him why he didn't severely discipline the horse, and John said simply, "He didn't mean it." By the next day, the horse had learned to stop without the use of force.

Under John's watchful eye, the elk herd in the "north end" flourished. He became legendary for his constant vigil and ability to endure all forms of weather. Asked in his later years about camping in blizzard conditions with few provisions, John stated, "winter never bothered me much then, I was sturdy enough." His Indian friends felt he could stand more cold than a coyote.

Just prior to retiring, John attended a training session at the newly established law enforcement academy. Part of the course involved physical training, and John, though twice the age of most trainees, would run an extra two or three laps after each session.

John's retirement income was a pittance, so he maintained six or eight horses and started a small outfitting business in his later years. But his game warden years were the zenith of his career, and when asked if he would do it again, his reply was "Yeah, I would. I prefer that to anything you can name."

A handmade buckskin jacket with bobcat trim that John Aeschbach made from a deer he shot with a primitive bow and arrow. He would wear the jacket for special occasions.
Photo courtesy of Jay Lawson.

John and Anna continued to live in their log cabin in semi-retirement—heating with wood and hauling water from the river. John kept a string of horses until the point in time when he entered a nursing home.

John Aeschbach passed away on August 12, 1977. The elk herd he established became his legacy, and Wyoming hunters owe him much.

Photo courtesy of Vickie Abbott.

14

Don Bell
Recollections of a Rodeo Cowboy and Big Game Hunter

During the first years of the 20th century, travel by horse remained a necessity in most western states. As the automobile became prevalent, those horsemen and horsewomen who had great talent continued to find ways to make a living on the back of a horse. Don Bell was such a man.

Don Bell was born on June 12, 1911 at his parent's homestead in eastern Colorado. Working outdoors and riding horses were part of everyday life, and from the earliest age Don took to it naturally.

His uncle was an early rancher in that country, and had contracts to breed horses for the cavalry; first the Cuban Army, then later the U.S. Cavalry. He would range breed his thoroughbred stud with Spanish Barb mustangs, thus producing a horse with great endurance as well as the dark colors and dark hooves insisted upon by the cavalry. Don learned much about horses from helping his uncle as a child.

Don had a natural affinity for horses and as he put it, was soon "ridin' everything I could get on." He entered his first rodeo at the age of twelve.

In that era, most young boys were expected to start working by the age of eleven or twelve, and many took jobs digging postholes as the open range was being fenced. It paid one dollar per day, working from dawn to dark. Don took one look at those operations and figured they weren't for him. He began trapping, running coyotes with hounds for a bounty, breaking horses and entering the earliest rodeos. Those pursuits paid far more than digging postholes. They also suited his adventurous spirit.

At the age of fifteen, Don joined an early Wild West show in Oklahoma, produced by Rufus Rollins. It was primarily a "bronc show," and the young cowboys would herd the horses from one town to another. They slept and cooked in the open and would simply put on their show in open fields or lots. With no chutes, the wild broncs were simply snubbed to a post until you could get on. Pretty Western!

In the winter, Don worked at the stockyards and spent his evenings at farrier school learning to shoe horses.

At sixteen, Don headed back to Colorado and joined the Bill King Rodeo Company. The King Ranch would be his

Don Bell was one of the earliest rodeo cowboys.
In the first years of the sport, a winning ride might pay $15.
Photo courtesy of Vickie Abbott.

headquarters off and on for years to come. Don would break horses for $7.50 a head and rodeo every weekend. By the time he reached his early twenties, he had "started winning" and was traveling to some big shows.

In 1935, Don bought a big old Nash automobile, and he and four other cowboys hit the rodeo circuit. They would camp wherever night found them, bathing in streams and shaving in the rearview mirror. A canvas tarp was used to form a lean-to on the side of the car, and they pitched their bedrolls under that. Whoever had a winning ride bought the beer and food.

Don was soon entering the largest rodeos, including Soldier's Field in Chicago and the Boston Gardens. But due to crooked promoters, there was little money to be made. As one fellow cowboy put it, "The only real hazard in riding bulls and broncs was starvin' to death."

In 1936, the top cowboys went on strike at the Boston Gardens, buying tickets and sitting in the stands. The promoters soon relented and purses for winners began to increase. The Turtle's Association was soon formed, a precursor of today's Professional Rodeo Cowboys Association (PRCA). Don was one of its earliest members.

During the late 1930s, numerous Hollywood Westerns were produced, and Don was hired to pack complete movie sets and entire casts into the Sierra Nevada mountains of California. He would then pack supplies in to the movie crew on a daily basis.

On one trip to a movie set, the director met Don as he rode into camp and advised they would not be filming that day as there was no stunt man available. Don thought for a moment, and then told him, "I'm about half stunt man, what do you need?" They soon struck a deal, and after dressing Don in a cavalry outfit complete with a saber, he had to ride a horse off a high ledge and into the pool of a river below. The director was thrilled with the action and wanted to try another take; Don declined.

Don had small parts in several Western movies including *Rose Marie* with Nelson Eddy and Jeanette McDonald, and *Shane*, filmed in Jackson Hole.

In 1943, Don entered the Army to serve in World War II. Having been a hunter all his life, he qualified as an expert marksman and was assigned to the 29th Infantry Division. Being one of the first units to land on Omaha Beach during the invasion of Normandy, the 29th experienced tremendous losses. Over two thousand American lives were lost on that beach alone.

Don survived the landing, and soon found himself in a foxhole with famed war correspondent Ernie Pyle. Ernie had heard of Don's colorful background, and they were drinking cognac and completing an interview when a German artillery shell landed nearby, covering Don, Ernie, and his portable typewriter with dirt. Ernie left the typewriter with Don, telling him "anyone that can tell stories like you should be a writer." Sadly, Ernie was later killed with the Marines just days before the war ended.

Don was wounded on July 12 near St. Lo, France, receiving gunshot wounds to the shoulder and ankle. Evacuated to the Normandy beachhead, he and approximately one hundred other wounded soldiers on stretchers were shelled as they lay on the beach. Don was hit in the jaw by a shell fragment; somehow he survived and was sent to England for surgery and a long recuperation.

Following the war, Don tried to reenter the rodeo circuit, but soon found that his war injuries limited his ability to compete. Never one to be held back, he soon headed to Cody, Wyoming, to pursue his love of hunting.

Establishing himself in Cody in 1946, Don was soon breaking horses, shoeing horses, and "selling whiskey on Sunday." He hired out as a wrangler and guide to famed outfitter Max Wilde from 1948-1952, and was soon proficient at finding elk, bear and sheep for his clients.

In 1953, actress Hope Williams of New York hired Don to run a hunting outfit from her ranch on the South Fork of the Shoshone River. Packing hunters and fishermen into the Absaroka wilderness added one more chapter to a life filled with adventure.

Don Bell with a great mule deer buck
taken in the Absaroka wilderness.
Photo courtesy of Vickie Abbott.

Grizzly bear hunting was still open during those years, and Don had several close calls with the big bears. When one client shot a grizzly at close range, Don cautioned him to "have a smoke" and wait to ensure the bear was dead. Rejecting that advice, the hunter approached the bear and touched his head with the muzzle of his rifle. The bear let out a loud roar and knocked the rifle into the air. Lucky for him, Don had his old lever-action .30-30 at hand and rushed forward to finish off the bear.

Packing the bear's hide out on his saddle horse, Don failed to realize that the grizzly's claws were raking his horse's flanks. He soon "went to buckin' " and carried Don off through the forest. Arriving at camp late, he was relieved to find that his hunter's horse had brought back the client safely.

In a humorous hunting anecdote, Don related the time that he had located a big mule deer buck for a hunter, and had situated the man along the path the buck used at first light. Sure enough, the big deer came down the trail, but when the hunter went to chamber a round he found that he had reached into his pocket for shells and loaded his stick of lip balm into the magazine. To say the least, the gun wouldn't function!

Among his hunting and fishing clients were several notable personalities, including Lee Marvin, John Armstrong, and actress Janet Gaynor. When Ms. Gaynor wanted to take home the skull and antlers from a large seven-point bull elk, Don tied it to her vehicle with a diamond hitch; it made quite a sight!

Through the years, Don had done some writing about his adventures, and the western magazines of that time purchased them. At the age of sixty-two, he made the decision

Don with a big grizzly bear.
The bear's claws began raking the flanks of his saddle horse
as he packed it out, and there was a small rodeo
right there in the wilderness.
Photo courtesy of Vickie Abbott.

to quit guiding and write full time. That was nearly thirty years ago, and at the age of ninety-two he is still being published.   Don lives today in the small town of Byron with his wife, Elvira. This past year he was inducted into the Cowboy Hall of Fame. He is also the only rodeo cowboy inducted into the Texas Rangers Sports Hall of Fame.

I interviewed Don at the home of his daughter, Vickie Abbott, in Meeteetse recently. His amazing stories ranged from the early rodeo days to his landing on Omaha Beach, then on to Cody for a hunting career and concluding with his years as a Western author. When we finished, I remarked that he had led quite a colorful and adventurous life. Don thought for a moment and remarked, "Yes, it's been quite a life."

Don Bell passed away on April 21, 2005.

Photo courtesy of Cal King.

15

Cal King
Game Warden, Biologist, Scholar

The period following World War II saw the emergence of modern wildlife management in Wyoming. It was a period of transition, and to succeed one had to be able to work with tough old game wardens from the early days as well as apply new scientific principles. Cal King was perfectly suited to that task.

Cal was born on April 19, 1921, in Fort Collins, Colorado. His father, Vernon King, moved the family to Edgerton, Wyoming when Cal was only three years old. The Teapot Dome oil boom was on, and Cal's father opened a second-hand furniture store, which was a great success.

Cal was only four years old when his mother, Elizabeth, contracted tuberculosis. Little was known about the disease in those days, and when his mother was confined to a Colorado sanatorium, he and his two brothers, Don and Gordon, were not allowed to visit her due to concerns over the disease being contagious. Unable to be with his mother as a young boy was traumatic and life-changing; Cal became self-reliant and independent in his thinking at that early age.

Cal was sent to live with Dr. Harry P. Scott, a Fort Collins veterinarian. Dr. Scott fostered an interest in learning which would serve Cal well in later years. He also encouraged Cal's natural affinity for both wild and domestic animals.

Returning to Wyoming when his mother was released from the hospital, Cal lived in Chugwater, Albin, and Saratoga where he attended high school. He was able to pursue his love of hunting and fishing in the upper Platte Valley; he also became an excellent student.

Graduating as the salutatorian of his high school class, Cal was offered several scholarships. He was also offered an appointment to the U.S. Naval Academy at Annapolis, being sponsored by Wyoming Senator Joseph C. O'Mahoney.

Knowing that Senator O'Mahoney enjoyed trout fishing, Cal went to the Sierra Madre Mountains and caught a limit of nice brook trout. He packed them in a wooden cooler and took them on the train as he headed for Washington D.C. It was 2001 miles from Saratoga to the nation's capital and Cal placed the fish in the pullman car's refrigeration unit so they would not spoil.

Arriving on the steps of the capitol with his cooler, Cal was stopped by Secret Service agents and questioned about his package. After seeing the fresh trout, the agents escorted him to the senator's office. Senator O'Mahoney was thrilled with the gift and invited a fellow congressman who was also an angler to dinner and they shared Cal's catch.

With the outbreak of World War II, the Naval Academy placed their students on an accelerated schedule; no newspapers, no radios, no movies, just studying. Obedience, manners, and courtesy were the order of the day, and those who know Cal well can attest to the fact that he has never lost those qualities.

Cal's father had built him a boxing ring when he was a boy and taught him how to punch. While attending the Naval Academy, he would win his weight class in boxing.

Attending flight school upon graduation, Cal was soon deployed to aircraft carriers in the far east. Though many friends were lost, Cal and his fellow naval aviators emerged victorious over seasoned Japanese pilots in aerial combat over the Pacific islands.

Returning from the war, Cal decided to pursue a second degree at Colorado A&M (now Colorado State University). After graduating from their zoology program, he enrolled in a masters degree program at the University of Wyoming. Upon graduation, he held three prestigious degrees, but being a lifelong learner, he would later obtain a degree in law and study entomology by correspondence through Purdue University.

While at the University of Wyoming, Cal met his future wife, Judy, and they were inseparable from that point on, Judy being not only his wife, but his best friend as well.

Cal King as a young Naval aviator.
Following graduation from the U.S. Naval Academy and flight school,
he flew fighters from carriers in the Pacific during World War II.
Photo courtesy of Cal King.

In 1949, Cal King went to work as a game warden for the Wyoming Game and Fish Department. In Cal's words, "I couldn't have got a better job." Following a short stint in Cokeville and Kemmerer, he was assigned as the district game warden in Thermopolis, replacing old-time game warden "Tennessee" Hall.

Cal King as the newly appointed Thermopolis game warden in 1950.
Photo courtesy of Cal King.

At that point in time, Cal was very likely the most educated game warden in America. Tennessee Hall was a real character, and thought he would show the young college grad a thing or two. He picked Cal up in his pickup with a frozen coyote sitting upright between them! He then proceeded to take him through the hills and ended up at an old cabin near dark. Rather than dinner, they had a few glasses of whiskey and then slept in the freezing cabin with only a single fencepost to burn in the cowboy stove.

Cal survived the indoctrination and went on to be a highly respected game warden in the Thermopolis district. Among those who befriended him was rancher Ramul

Cal and a fellow game warden "goin' to the hills."
Cal never went on patrol without one of his dogs,
some of which were highly trained to assist him
in law enforcement or animal capture.
Photo courtesy of Cal King.

Dvarishkis, the first person featured in this series. Ramul outfitted Cal with a fine Morgan horse and taught him how to get along in the high country.

Tennessee Hall had told Cal, "You're going to have a tough time," as illegal hunting was common around Thermopolis. Cal seized eleven deer during his first patrol in the Copper Mountain area. The word soon went out that such poaching would not be tolerated, and violations diminished greatly.

During one patrol up the Owl Creek drainage, Cal and Sheriff Eddie Todorovich apprehended a fugitive who was hiding out at an old ranch. He was on the FBI's Ten Most Wanted list.

In 1956, Cal was appointed as the first wildlife biologist in the Bighorn Basin. He immediately began an inventory of big game habitat, establishing vegetation transects and photo-points in crucial ranges. He was one of the first wildlife managers in the West to begin relating harvest management and herd size to forage availability and the health of plant communities. In later years, he would donate his extensive herbarium to the University of Wyoming.

While conducting his range surveys, Cal built a small packsaddle for his dog, and his best friend would carry the instruments for measuring vegetation. He trained a second and much smaller dog to enter bank dens of beaver so he could flush them out and capture them for relocation to areas where they had been extirpated.

Always an advocate for wildlife, Cal fought off several Desert Land Entry proposals to convert public big game winter ranges to private land.

Cal, with an orphaned fawn antelope,
had a natural rapport with both wild and domestic animals.
Photo courtesy of Cal King.

As Cal's knowledge of plants and attendant insect communities grew, he was asked to speak around the country, including a talk at the World's Fair in Seattle.

Through time, Cal developed an abiding interest in the history of wildlife conservation. He interviewed many of the old game wardens, cowboys and trappers still around in those days, including "High-power" Williams, who gained fame through killing the notorious Custer and Splitrock wolves. Cal eventually published three books on his findings: *Reestablishing Elk in the Bighorn Mountains of Wyoming*, *Reasons for the Decline of Game in the Bighorn Basin of Wyoming*, and *History of Wildlife in the Bighorn Basin of Wyoming*.

When it came to philanthropy, Cal's motto has always been "the more you give, the more you get back." In the 1960s, he hosted a fundraiser for crippled children and raised eighteen thousand dollars.

Being a highly successful investor, Cal eventually came to own several properties, including the land above Thermopolis between Roundtop Mountain and the Hot Springs State Park. It is a beautiful spot, and after his wife Judy passed away, he built a memorial to her in one of several small canyons. He often goes there to contemplate and observe plants and animals, which remain undisturbed.

Realizing that this wonderful piece of land would surely be developed and its intrinsic values destroyed by trophy homes built to satisfy some inflated ego, he asked me and former game warden Tim Britt to work with him to protect the property. Cal granted a conservation easement to the Nature Conservancy, and the mule deer, least chipmunks, chukar partridge, mountain lions, and other species will be able to live there in perpetuity.

Following retirement, Cal continued to hunt and fish, taking a deer and antelope at age seventy-nine. He also made two trips to the high arctic, including a prolonged stay at Guise Fiord, the northern most community in Canada. While there, he went out hunting marine mammals with the Inuit (Eskimo) who live there. He also inspected their ancient polar bear traps.

Despite Cal's success in the financial arena, he continues to live a modest existence. He is still learning, studying history and science, and he invented a modern skunk trap, which received a patent. His interest in animals is maintained through his prize homing pigeons, which he flies around the Bighorn Basin.

Cal King has served as a mentor to me, inspiring my interest in the history of wildlife management and encouraging me to write when possible. He should also serve as a role model to all of us in these relatively confusing times; his examples of courtesy, selflessness, and dedication to preserving Wyoming's natural qualities are rare traits we should return to.

Joe and Mary at their dude ranch near Dubois.
Photo courtesy of Wind River Valley Artists' Guild.

16

Joe and Mary Back
The Cowboy Meets a Lady

Once in a great while you find a man and woman united in a relationship of near total compatibility. At once friends and lovers, partners and soulmates and, in the rarest instance, sharing interests and vocations. Joe and Mary Back of Dubois, Wyoming were such a couple.

Joe Back was born April 12, 1899, in Montpelier, Ohio. His father was a country doctor who visited his patients by horse and buggy. A lover of horses, he maintained a breeding stable when not practicing medicine. Through him, Joe developed knowledge of horses at the earliest age, handling the buggy as his father made his rounds.

When Joe was only nine years old his father died of a sudden heart attack. His mother relocated to California where she soon remarried. Joe could not get along with his stepfather who was quite a drinker; so when he got in trouble at school for drawing sketches of his eighth grade teacher, he decided that was enough of that whole situation and took off on his own.

Joe's mother had a cousin who managed the Fiddleback Ranch north of Douglas, so Joe headed there and was put to work as a chore-boy for board and room. Having learned to handle horses from his father, he was soon promoted to full ranch hand status with wages of forty-five dollars a month.

With the onset of World War I, Joe entered the Navy. Proficient with firearms, he was assigned to be a machine gun instructor and the closest thing to an ocean he ever saw was Lake Michigan. Discharged in 1919, Joe returned to Douglas and began cowboying on the 55 Ranch for ranch foreman Wheeler Eskew. Wheeler was a top hand and Joe considered him "one of the finest men I ever got to know."

Joe had filed on a homestead forty-two miles north of Douglas and had begun the improvements necessary to obtain full ownership when he heard about a big horse roundup. Hiring on with six or eight other cowboys, they eventually caught several hundred stray horses, which were to be purchased by the Diamond G Guest ranch above Dubois. They then obtained a chuck wagon and rope corral and herded the horses from Douglas to Brooks Lake and the Diamond G, a distance of approximately 270 miles. The trip took two weeks and was filled with adventure.

The Diamond G wanted Joe to stay on as a wrangler and guide, so he leased the grass on his homestead and remained in the mountains. He began guiding summer pack trips in the Teton Wilderness, including trips as far as Lewis Lake in Yellowstone National Park. In the fall, he would guide elk, deer, and bighorn sheep hunters.

Joe Back had always liked to draw and sketch and the Brooks Lake country was full of subject material. He began making sketches of horses, mountains, and cowboys and gave them away to ranch guests. One summer-long guest was Louis Agassiz Fuertes, a staff artist with *National Geographic*. When he saw Joe's sketches, he encouraged him to attend the Art Institute of Chicago.

Initially rejected because he had only completed the eighth grade, Joe figured that was the end of that idea. But when Fuertes found out about it, he gathered up Joe's sketches and sent them to the Institute with a strongly worded letter; Joe was accepted. He quickly sold his homestead and headed east. It was at the Art Institute of Chicago that Joe would meet his future wife and lifelong partner.

Mary Waters Cooper was born on Dec. 3, 1906 in Minneapolis, Minnesota. While still an infant, her father moved the family to Vermont. Even as a young child, Mary's interests in nature and art were evident. Her notebooks would be festooned with drawings, often of plants or animals. Her father was a member of the Green Mountain Club, which established hiking trails reaching to Canada, so Mary spent weekends hiking the hills and clearing trails. Early pictures show Mary with various animals, including several pet snakes.

Joe and Mary Back
ready to depart the Art Institute of Chicago for Wyoming in 1935.
Photo courtesy of Wind River Valley Artists' Guild.

Graduating from high school at the age of sixteen, Mary was admitted to Berea College in Kentucky. A small, prestigious school, Berea charged no tuition but required students to hold jobs at the college. When Mary arrived, she brought one of her pet snakes which caused quite a commotion and was eventually placed in the biology lab.

While Mary was at college, her family relocated to Chicago. Joining them there following graduation, she began taking classes at the Art Institute of Chicago. Classes in animal anatomy were held at the Field Museum of Natural

Mary hunting after a fresh snow.
Photo courtesy of Wind River Valley Artists' Guild.

History, and one day while Mary was sketching animals, someone walked up behind her and remarked, "That's a helluva good bear!" It was Joe Back.

Joe courted Mary during 1931 and 1932, and they finally married in February of 1933, during the Great Depression. Jobs were scarce, but Joe was hired as a foreman by the National Park Service for $175 a month, and Mary was appointed to run a trailside wildlife museum for one hundred dollars per month. They lived on Joe's salary and saved Mary's earnings with a plan to move to Wyoming.

In the spring of 1935, Joe and Mary bought a 1927 Buick to make the trip west. They sewed a canvas tent which could be affixed to the side of the car and camped their way through the country, arriving at Dubois, Wyoming, Joe's old stomping ground.

Moving to the high country, Mary and Joe purchased the abandoned and dilapidated Lava Creek Ranch. Working nearly around the clock, they rendered the ranch cabins ready for winter. And that first winter was a tough one with deep snow and cold temperatures. Joe would take two days to snowshoe the twenty-two miles to Dubois for the mail and a few groceries. But they both decided to stick it out.

Given her somewhat genteel and urban background, it is amazing how much Mary took to Wyoming's wildlands. Her sentiments are perfectly reflected in a short essay to the Berea College alumni newsletter, where she spoke of her first winter in the wilderness.

"Sheer beauty. It is a privilege to just be in a world so lovely, so bright with changing color; so rich in the detail of

How To Tie the Diamond Hitch
Joe's sketches enhanced the popularity of his horse-packing publications.
Photo courtesy of Wind River Valley Artists' Guild.

bird and animal form and action, and the patterning of the lodgepoles and the willows; so tremendous in the massing of the great mountains; so aloof and remote from the smoke and fussiness of human crowding."

Then later, *"There is a relief to all one's senses at the lessened feeling of being just a cog in a great, impersonal, and intricate Society, the relief and responsibility of being 'on your own' for better or for worse."*

And in closing, *"I have actually heard this vivid, beautiful, ever-changing country called 'God-forsaken.' We both find it in our hearts to thank God that it is so comparatively human-forsaken."*

Mary and Joe ran the Lava Creek Ranch as a dude outfit for nearly four years. These were lean times, calling for improvisation and doing it yourself. Mary learned to do carpentry, dig ditches, butcher elk, and skin beaver. During the fall, Joe would be gone for weeks on end guiding hunters, and in her journals Mary speaks of how lonely she became without him; truly an inseparable pair.

They later sold Lava Creek Ranch and bought the Rocker Y, another dude ranch, but a bigger operation. While they loved the lifestyle, it did not allow them the time they needed to pursue their art careers. After a long day in the saddle or a day spent cooking and cleaning, their creative energies for painting and drawing were diminished.

During World War II, Joe and Mary worked for the war effort in California; Joe as a shipyard welder, and Mary as an airplane mechanic. Returning to Dubois at war's end, they dude ranched for one more year.

By the spring of 1946, Joe and Mary came to realize that they would never become full-time artists running a hectic dude outfit. They sold the Rocker Y, moved east of Dubois and built a cabin that would also serve as an art studio.

Drawing and sculpting did not pay all the bills, so Joe took odd jobs, including stints with the Wyoming Game and Fish Department as a seasonal game warden and packing fish into the wilderness for stocking. He also continued guiding hunters and always got his own elk for the winter's meat—a staple since the Lava Creek days.

Joe published a small pamphlet on horse packing, *How To Tie a Diamond Hitch*, illustrated with his colorful sketches. It was in big demand, so he launched a book project to produce

Mary working on sculptures in Back's studio house.
Photo courtesy of Wind River Valley Artists' Guild.

Joe with sculpture of horse packing,
one of his favorite interests as well as art subjects.
Photo courtesy of Wind River Valley Artists' Guild.

a "horse packer's bible." The end product was *Horses, Hitches and Rocky Trails*, still in print and considered one of the best guides to horse packing in existence. His last chapters advocate respecting the wilderness and taking care of the mountain country. He would later publish several other books, and Mary would publish *Seven Half-Miles From Home*, a reminiscence of her walks in the upper Wind River country.

The University of Wyoming asked Mary to teach extension art classes, and she was soon teaching in Dubois, Lander, Crowheart and Riverton. Her classes were immensely popular, and the annual art show she arranged for her students and regional artists gave rise to the Wind River Valley Artists' Guild. Her efforts were later recognized when she received the Governor's Award for Service to the Arts. In addition, both she and Joe were awarded the Medallion of Honor by Central Wyoming College in 1982.

The Backs celebrated their 50th wedding anniversary in 1983, and over two hundred people arrived at their small studio home. This turnout portrayed the public's appreciation for all of Joe and Mary's community service.

Joe Back passed away on September 7, 1986. This was a terrific blow to Mary—she had lost her husband, best friend, and lifelong partner in all affairs. Despite the loss, Mary continued her work with the Wind River Valley Artists' Guild and maintained her habit of walking and bird watching along the Wind River, but she had lost much of her desire to paint with Joe's passing.

Mary Back died on May 28, 1991, but the legacy of Joe and Mary Back lives on through their artwork, writings and in the fond memories of countless friends.

The Wind River Valley Artists' Guild is now housed in the beautiful Headwaters Arts and Conference Center in Dubois. Visitors can enjoy the artwork of Joe and Mary Back as well as many other fine artists.

Photo courtesy of Nancy Corsi.

16

S.N. Leek
Father of the Elk

Perhaps the most ardent conservationists of the late nineteenth century were the frontiersmen who witnessed the loss of Wyoming's vast herds of big game. Stephen Nelson Leek was a classic of this type.

S.N. Leek was born in Turkey Point, Ontario, on April 23, 1858, the son of a Welsh farmer. One of his earliest recollections was the sight of immense flocks of passenger pigeons blocking out the sun. The rapid extinction of that species was said to have profoundly influenced his thinking and inspired a conservation ethic that would last a lifetime.

To place S.N. Leek's childhood in the context of his

time, it is interesting to note that during his first day of school, the teacher was sobbing at her desk. After finally gaining her composure, she informed the class that President Lincoln had been assassinated in Ford's Theater in Washington the night before.

S.N.'s father died when he was ten years old. His mother soon remarried, and moved to Illinois, where S.N. attended public schools. In his late teens, he relocated to Buffalo County, Nebraska, where he ran a small ranch.

While in Nebraska during the early 1880s, S.N., as he became known, witnessed the demise of remnant bison herds and the shipping of tons of buffalo bones and skulls to the East, probably to manufacture lime. This was another pivotal experience, further impressing upon his mind the need for wildlife conservation.

Around 1882, S.N. sold his small Nebraska ranch and headed to Wyoming. He hunted, trapped and cowboyed for a time in the northern Bighorn Mountains, and an old cabin with the carving, "S.N. Leek, 1882," bears witness to his having been at Shell Canyon during that time. That cabin and inscription are now at Old Trail Town in Cody.

Around 1888, S.N. traveled by horseback through Sunlight Basin and the Yellowstone country, arriving at Jackson's Lake, Wyoming Territory. Years later, he would describe that journey, including the abundance and diversity of wildlife and Indian burial grounds, in a popular article titled, *Early Days in the Yellowstone*.

S.N. passed the winter of 1888-89 on Jackson Lake with fellow hunter and trapper Nicholas Gass. It is said that S.N. fell in love with the grandeur and wildlife of Jackson Hole

An undeveloped Jackson Hole brimming with elk.
Leek used his photographs to promote creation of the National Elk Refuge.
Photo courtesy of Nancy Corsi.

and resolved to remain in that country.

S.N. trapped and hunted through his first year in the Hole, saving enough money to purchase a small ranch south of the fledgling town of Jackson. He kept a few cows, but ran the place primarily as a dude ranch and hunting outfit. In 1889, there were forty settlers in Jackson Hole; two years later there were one hundred.

In 1896, S.N. Leek met and married Etta Wilson, daughter of colorful "Uncle" Nick Wilson, for whom the town of Wilson is named. Uncle Nick had a colorful past—having lived with the Shoshone Indian tribe and later being a noted Pony Express rider. The characters in two books, *Uncle Nick Among the Shoshones* and *The White Indian Boy* were drawn from his life.

One of S.N.'s summer guests was George Eastman, who had founded much of the early photographic industry. He gave S.N. a camera when he was leaving, which launched a long career as a wildlife and nature photographer.

Stephen Leek became increasingly alarmed over the plight of elk in Jackson Hole. As ancient migration corridors were blocked and native meadows were hayed, the elk began to experience a great die-off. During harsh winters such as 1908, S.N. began photographing the starving animals and formed plans to remedy the situation.

In 1907, S.N. Leek was elected to represent Uinta County in the Wyoming Legislature (Teton County later was carved out of the original Uinta County). His primary goal in seeking office was to enact legislation benefiting the elk of Jackson Hole.

At that time, the Benevolent and Protective Order of Elks used elk teeth or "tusks" as emblems and symbols. With pairs of teeth commanding up to eighty-five dollars, many elk were being wantonly shot for their teeth by "tusk hunters." S.N. introduced a legislative resolution encouraging the abandonment of such practices by the Order, and the group subsequently stopped. In addition, the people of Jackson Hole held a mass meeting and gave the tusk hunters forty-eight hours to get out of the valley. They left in twenty-four hours, fearing a possible lynching.

Leek's next order of business was to procure five

The Leek Ranch in the early years.
Photo courtesy of Nancy Corsi.

thousand dollars in state funding to feed the elk in Jackson Hole. In order to secure more permanent federal funding, S.N. hit the lecture circuit with his dramatic photographs.

S.N. Leek, spent ten weeks on the Orpheum lecture circuit relaying the plight of his favorite elk herd. He spoke in New York City and Washington, D.C. The president and senators heard his plea, as well as George Eastman, famed photographer William H. Jackson and Gilbert Grosvenor, editor of *National Geographic*.

S.N. also was a prolific and talented writer, and his

stories and photographs regularly were seen in the earliest issues of *Outdoor Life* and other sporting publications. His literally was a one-man campaign to preserve the elk of Jackson Hole.

Primarily due to the individual actions of S.N. Leek, Congress appropriated funds to purchase 1,760 acres of land along Flat Creek. Combined with 1,040 acres of untouched public land, this parcel was dedicated as the National Elk Refuge. Subsequent land donations by the Izaak Walton League and John D. Rockefeller expanded the refuge to more than 23,000 acres. Newspaper reports concerning the refuge's dedication in 1912 christened S.N. Leek "Father of the Elk."

In 1924, at the age of sixty-seven, S.N. Leek decided to build a lodge and marina on his beloved Jackson Lake. He and his two sons, Lester and Holly (short for Holiday, as he was born on Christmas day), began construction. They felled their own logs and brought in a portable sawmill to cut their own lumber. Wanting to build a unique fireplace, they constructed a platform between two boats and hauled large rocks from across the lake. The lodge design was produced by S.N. himself.

In the early years, many affluent guests would stay at Leek's Lodge for the entire summer. Resident anglers could procure a boat and guide for a dollar an hour. In addition, many big game hunting trips were outfitted by the Leeks, some lasting a month or more.

In his later years, S.N. Leek spent his time recording memories of the early days in Jackson Hole and organizing his extensive photo collection. These priceless artifacts eventually would be housed at the University of Wyoming and the

S.N. Leek at the fireplace in Leek's Lodge.
The rocks for the fireplace were hauled by boat across Jackson Lake.
Photo courtesy of Nancy Corsi.

Jackson Hole Historical Society and Museum.

S.N. Leek passed away in 1943 at the age of eighty-five. As a pioneer conservationist, he had single-handedly protected the open space of much of Jackson Hole, and he preserved the elk herd that was so dear to his heart. We owe him a great deal.

Leek in his later years.
He began construction of Leek's Lodge at age sixty-seven.
Photo courtesy of Nancy Corsi.

Photo courtesy of Wyoming State Archives,
Department of State Parks and Cultural Resources.

18

D.C. Nowlin
Frontier Peace Officer and Pioneer Conservationist
The Man Who Shaped
Wyoming's Wildlife Management

Wyoming's wildlife was in desperate straits at the end of the 1890s. The buffalo were all but eliminated, antelope were vanishing from the prairies, and elk and mountain sheep had been extirpated in entire mountain ranges. It would take an old-time Western lawman of great vision to turn that situation around.

Daniel Crispin Nowlin was born on September 1, 1857, the son of James Crispin Nowlin and Ann Elizabeth

Nowlin. He was the first child born in Kerr County, Texas, after the county was formed. His father was a physician and surgeon in the famed Texas Rangers.

After attending public schools in Center Point, Texas, "D.C.," as he became known, worked as a surveyor and mineral prospector in both Texas and Old Mexico.

Following in his father's footsteps, D.C. next enlisted in the Texas Rangers at the age of sixteen. Joining the rangers in 1873 was a perilous decision for such a young man, as gunplay was a common occurrence on the frontier.

D.C. served in both A and F companies of the Frontier Battalion, Texas Rangers, which had been formed by a legislative act in 1874. The unit was created to combat raiding Comanche and Kiowa Indians, Mexican bandits and "other marauding or thieving parties."

Armed to the teeth, the rangers rarely went anywhere without a pair of Colt Peacemaker pistols, a lever-action rifle and a Bowie or Green River knife. It was a wild era, and the Frontier Battalion engaged in both mounted and dismounted gun battles with outlaws and Indians, often temporarily binding their prisoners to trees due to a lack of jail facilities.

Mustering out of the rangers, D.C. returned to surveying for a time and also worked as editor of a newspaper. Tiring of that life, he headed to Rio Grande City to participate in the roundup of more than four thousand Texas longhorns.

D.C. and a band of cowboys began driving this great herd up the old trail to Montana, including a sojourn in Dodge City, then famous as a cow town. His later notes would show they encountered wild buffalo and he shot two bison near the Tongue River on the Wyoming and Montana territorial

Company F, Frontier Battalion, Texas Rangers.
Nowlin rode with this outfit years before this picture was taken.
Photo courtesy of Western History Collections,
University of Oklahoma Libraries.

boundary. It was a great adventure, a real-life version of
Lonesome Dove character Augustus (Gus) McCrae, right
down to the fact that Gus was a former Texas Ranger.

D.C. next relocated to Lincoln County, New Mexico,
then one of the largest and wildest counties in the West. Pat
Garrett, Lincoln County Sheriff, had recently killed Billy the
Kid, but numerous outlaws remained at large.

Early Lincoln County records show that D.C. Nowlin
was elected superintendent of schools in 1886, receiving 552
votes. Subsequently, he decided to run for sheriff, with his

Dan Nowlin participated in one of the great cattle drives from Texas to Montana.
Photo courtesy of Wyoming State Archives, Department of State Parks and Cultural Resources.

Texas Ranger credentials solidly behind him. He was elected to a two-year term in 1888, and was able to continue the work of Pat Garrett and other frontier peace officers who were trying to bring law and order to an area once declared to be in a "state of insurrection."

Current Lincoln County Sheriff Tom Sullivan visited with me about the late 1880s in that country, and felt sure that Nowlin would have had occasion to work with Pat Garrett, who was then a lawman in nearby Doña Ana County.

While in Lincoln County, D.C. Nowlin married Laura Nancy Leonard, with whom he eventually would have five children: Bryan, Percy, Bruce, Bernice and Prentiss.

D.C. had enjoyed Wyoming when he passed through the state during the big cattle drive. Selling his holdings in Texas and New Mexico, he made a decision to start a cattle ranch west of Big Piney. He also operated a ranch near Dubois later on.

Appalled by the continued decline of game animals, Nowlin decided to run for the Fifth Wyoming Legislature in 1899. Once elected, he immediately drafted a comprehensive game protection act—establishing actual seasons for hunting, imposing harvest limits and creating the position of State Game Warden. The bill also restricted the take of fish and defined legal fishing tackle.

Nowlin's work in the legislature created the foundation for a sound conservation program; he literally could be described as the father of Wyoming wildlife management.

In 1902, Albert Nelson resigned as State Game Warden, frustrated over his inability to get even a single conviction from local courts. Dan Nowlin was appointed to the position, and he approached the job with determination, stating: "Conservation is not only morally right, but a good financial investment for ourselves and our posterity."

Innovation was the hallmark of D.C. Nowlin's eight year career as State Game Warden. One of his first goals was to establish a fund for managing wildlife. Imposing hunting and fishing license fees would serve "the double purpose of restricting hunting and creating a game fund." His endeavors paid off and the system of wildlife funding we have today was born.

In 1903, D.C. Nowlin could only hire three full-time salaried game wardens. Stretching his budget, he hired twenty "special assistant" wardens for expense reimbursement only, several others who worked purely as volunteers, and he also deputized numerous forest rangers and national park rangers. The result was an adequate force to begin turning the tide on illegal hunting.

Nowlin was no armchair administrator, and in his 1903 report he states, "I have tried to visit in person the principal game sections of the state, and during the present year have visited or passed through eleven counties. I rode constantly in the counties of Uinta, Fremont, and Bighorn, where most of the elk and antelope are found, traveling more than one thousand miles on horseback."

It is hard to imagine just how many miles Dan Nowlin rode horseback in his life. Just prior to his thousand-mile hunting season patrol, he had taken his family on a horse and wagon trip from Big Piney through Jackson Hole and Yellowstone National Park.

By 1905, "tusk hunters" were killing large numbers of elk for their teeth, and Nowlin finally went to the legislature and asked that a felony statute be developed to address the "lawless vagabonds" who were killing big game for their antlers and tusks. The new law, combined with the abandonment of practices utilizing elk teeth by the Benevolent and Protective Order of Elks, turned the situation around.

In addition to the concept of licensed hunters and anglers funding wildlife management, Nowlin also created one of the first harvest reporting systems. Each hunter who killed a big game animal had to "detach at once a proper coupon and forward the same by mail to D.C. Nowlin, State Game Warden, Lander, Wyoming." Harvest figures could now be obtained and replaced earlier guesstimates.

Through D.C. Nowlin, Wyoming was forging a wildlife management policy that would become a model for the entire country. As Nowlin put it, "Game protection in Wyoming has passed the experimental stage and is now the recognized policy of the state."

Nowlin's system of wildlife management and conservation was for the benefit of all citizens; thus, it was in stark contrast to European management which favored the wealthy and those with titles.

The first translocation of elk from Jackson Hole to areas of extirpation was directed by Nowlin. The elk were trapped and taken by wagon and sleigh over Teton Pass to the railhead at St. Anthony, Idaho, then taken by train to Sheridan. Of the twenty-eight elk with which they began, twenty were released in the foothills of the Big Horn

Mountains. This Herculean task would set the stage for future transplants, with elk from Jackson Hole providing a source which repopulated elk herds in many western states, another first for D.C. Nowlin.

Nowlin served as state game warden through 1910. He had accomplished his personal goal of turning around the decline of fish and game in Wyoming. Trout were once again abundant in most streams, deer were increasing, elk were being restored and antelope had been saved from near extinction.

Dan Nowlin then began his next adventure, being appointed first director of the newly created National Elk

D.C. Nowlin overseeing the dissection of a diseased elk.
Photo courtesy of Wyoming State Archives,
Department of State Parks and Cultural Resources.

Refuge. He had that position for several years and also served as a justice of the peace in the recently formed Teton County.

D.C. Nowlin developed health problems in the early 1920s and returned to Kerr County, Texas, where his mother was still living. She passed away on Feb. 1, 1925, and D.C. followed her in death two months later on March 30, 1925.

Today, Daniel C. Nowlin is buried in a frontier cemetery in Center Point, Texas. A Texas state historical sign proclaims that there are thirty-two Texas Rangers buried there, listing D.C. as well as his father, J.C. Nowlin.

D.C. Nowlin led an incredible life, filled with adventure and accomplishment. He was a Western Renaissance man who arrived on the scene just in time to save many wildlife populations from certain extirpation. His daring and enterprise were employed to further the public good with no expectation of personal reward—an uncommon virtue today.

Perhaps the epitaph on D.C. Nowlin's tombstone sums him up, "Daniel C. Nowlin, Pioneer and Patriot. He feared nothing on earth and had no dread of the hereafter."

Photo courtesy of Tony Simon.

19

James R. Simon
Biologist and Cinematographer

Among my fellow fish and wildlife managers, James R. Simon is known for his pioneering work on the fish of Wyoming. He literally introduced ecological principles into our fisheries program, and he is held in high regard by today's biologists. But there is much more to this complex man of science, his life history being one of the most fascinating I have had the pleasure to explore.

Jim Simon was born in North Platte, Nebraska, on Feb. 13, 1908. His father had a tinsmithing business, and when Jim was ten the family transported their entire machine shop by rail to Riverton, Wyoming. Jim was the oldest of four

Jim's boyhood experiences hunting and fishing
in Wyoming inspired him to seek careers in
biology and wildlife cinematography.
Photo courtesy of Tony Simon.

sons and two daughters, and he and his brother, Felix, took an instant liking to the outdoor life Fremont County had to offer. Hunting, fishing and outdoor sports, particularly swimming and ice skating, were part of everyday life.

Jim and Felix became amateur naturalists while in their teens, and both decided to pursue degrees in zoology. Studying together under Dr. John Scott at the University of Wyoming, they both obtained masters degrees doing research on diseases and parasites of Wyoming fishes. In addition to being an honor student, Jim also was a member of the college swim team. At about this time, they both became early Wyoming members of the American Fisheries Society.

Felix elected to attend medical school while Jim stayed on to teach zoology at the university for two years. While there, he met and married his wife, Dorothy.

Longing for the outdoor life, Jim next took an assignment as a ranger and naturalist in Yellowstone National Park in 1936. His work studying the distribution of fish species in the Park led to an appointment with the U.S. Bureau of Fisheries and his subsequent publication of *Yellowstone Fishes*.

In 1937, the Wyoming Game and Fish Department was reorganized under Dr. John Scott. He appointed Jim as Wyoming State Fish Commissioner and State Fish Warden. Jim immediately undertook a complete inventory of Wyoming fishes, disposed of several obsolete hatcheries and introduced scientific concepts to many old-time fisheries personnel. Though somewhat controversial, his changes soon improved operations and he became well-respected throughout the state.

Jim was a pioneer fisheries scientist in Wyoming,
writing both *Yellowstone Fishes* and *Wyoming Fishes.*
Photo courtesy of Tony Simon.

With the outbreak of World War II, Jim joined the Navy and was commissioned a lieutenant. Initially sent to Columbia University to prepare for Pentagon duty, he was later assigned to the Pacific Theater as the war intensified.

The Army prevailed upon the Navy to loan Jim to the 7th Army under General Simon Buckner's command. His assignment was to study fish populations as potential food sources for natives and American troops. After the general's death at Okinawa, Jim remained on as fisheries officer for the Pacific Command.

Felix and Jim Simon, third and fourth from left,
at an early fisheries camp in the mountains.
Photo courtesy of Tony Simon.

Jim's swimming and diving skills were invaluable during his stint in the Pacific. During one diving expedition, Jim and his assistants had been underwater for an extended period of time, and when they surfaced, it was discovered that a rapidly moving typhoon had caused extensive damage to their boats and the island.

At the close of the war, Jim left naval service with the rank of lieutenant commander. He returned to Wyoming and the Game and Fish Department.

Jim had begun studying photography in college, and had continued to hone his skills with both still and motion picture equipment during his time in the military. Upon his return to Wyoming, he began filming wildlife and would often show his films during Game and Fish public meetings. One of his first film productions was *Wyoming's Big Game*, and it revealed his artistic talent and his eye for photographing wildlife.

Jim published his definitive *Wyoming Fishes* in 1946, and that text is still in use today. In the foreword, he explains his intent in producing this work:

It is not intended for the advanced ichthyologist, but rather for the student and fisherman and all other conservation-minded individuals who desire a general knowledge and understanding of this valuable wild resource, with a view to its conservation and proper use. If information contained herein enriches the fishing pleasure of any person, if it imparts a broader knowledge and understanding of Wyoming fishes and the problems relating thereto—and if in accomplishing this it furnishes some foundation on which future management of Wyoming's

Jim Simon with daughter, Nini, in the Amazon
filming the jaguar documentary *Jungle Cat*.
Photo courtesy of Tony Simon.

fisheries resources can be based—this volume will have fulfilled the purpose for which it is offered.

In 1947, Jim accepted an appointment as director of the Jackson Hole Wildlife Park and the New York Zoological Society's Field Station located near Moran.

The Jackson Hole assignment allowed Jim to perfect his film-making skills, and his short films soon came to the attention of Walt Disney. Disney later offered Jim a contract as field director and cinematographer for Walt Disney Productions.

Jim soon rose to prominence in the world of nature documentaries. Many motion pictures were shot at least partially in Wyoming, with *Beaver Valley* winning early acclaim. His *Vanishing Prairie* and *The Living Desert* both won Academy Awards, as did *Bear Country* and *Water Birds*. He would spend nearly two years in the far north of Canada shooting *White Wilderness*, and it, too, won an Academy Award.

Assignments with Disney took Jim around the world. In order to film the jaguar documentary *Jungle Cat*, he moved his wife, Dorothy, daughter, Nini, and son, Tony, to Brazil and the Amazon for more than two years. That movie would win Filmdom's Famous Fives Award.

After nine years of filming with Disney, Jim left to produce an African documentary for the New York Zoological Society. The intent of the film was to portray conflicts between cattle and native African wildlife.

Following his African expedition, Jim decided to relocate his family back in Wyoming. He was hired as special projects director by the Wyoming Travel Commission in Cheyenne.

Jim Simon in the Canadian arctic
filming *White Wilderness*, which won an Academy Award.
Photo courtesy of Tony Simon.

Jim immediately began creating a series of publications and television spots promoting Wyoming's outdoor amenities. His stunning photography literally *made* those brochures, books and films.

In 1971, Jim received the prestigious National Press Photographers Association Television News Film Award.

Jim Simon's life would be cut short by lung cancer in 1973. It is incredible to think of what he had accomplished in sixty-five years. His achievements in the dual fields of biology and cinematography are astounding. Perhaps no other person has done more to promote an appreciation of Wyoming's wildlife and wild lands.

In a personal note a year before his death, Wyoming Senator Clifford Hansen wrote to Jim, "Few people have done more unusual things than you, and fewer still have contributed so much to a state and nation."

Photo courtesy of Buffalo Bill Historical Center,
Cody, Wyoming.
Gift of Mr. and Mrs. Charles Belden; P.67.1002.

20

Charles J. Belden
Cowboy Photographer

Readers may not be familiar with the name Charles Belden, but most would recognize his distinctive photographs of early 20th century Wyoming ranch life. The compositions are so striking that they stick in your memory and you begin to recognize his unique style just as you would a talented painter.

Charles Josiah Belden was born in San Francisco on Nov. 26, 1887 to a quite prominent family. His grandfather and namesake, Josiah Belden, had been part of the famous Donner Party, a group migrating west that got trapped in the Sierra Nevada mountains during the winter of 1846-47.

Belden carefully created many scenes.
Note the head of the cowboy's horse.
Photo courtesy of Wyoming State Archives,
Department of State Parks and Cultural Resources.

Nearly half of the party died, and some resorted to eating their dead to survive. Josiah Belden was highly successful in developing real estate when the city was built. His father, Charles Albert Belden, became successful in the hardware business.

Charles was a bright and creative student, and in 1906 was accepted to the Massachusetts Institute of Technology. While at MIT, he became close friends with Eugene Phelps, whose family owned the beautiful Pitchfork Ranch west of Meeteetse.

In 1909, Charles, along with Eugene Phelps and Stanley Page, decided to tour Europe. The three shipped over a 1908 Packard touring car, and soon were visiting Italy, Germany, France and Austria. They even entered Russia for a time, a rare event for an American in that era.

While in Germany, Charles purchased a high-quality Zeiss camera, which had a shutter speed adjusting to 1/1,000 of a second. Upon returning to America, he began to teach himself every aspect of photography, including development of glass negatives and enlarging prints.

Charles Belden accompanied his close friend Eugene to Wyoming and the Pitchfork Ranch following graduation. He immediately fell in love with both the country and with Eugene's sister, Frances. They soon were married.

The Pitchfork Ranch had been created by German nobleman Count Otto Franc (the town of Otto and Franc's Peak are named after him). It subsequently was purchased by Eugene's father, Louis Graham Phelps. The ranch was eventually built up to include nearly 250,000 acres and is generally considered one of the most scenic ranches in North America.

The cowboy with a mule deer buck
captures the essence of high country hunting.
*Photo courtesy of Wyoming State Archives,
Department of State Parks and Cultural Resources.*

Long Trail Winding,
one of Charles Belden's signature photographs,
exemplifying his artistic style and eye for composition.
Photo courtesy of Buffalo Bill Historical Center, Cody, Wyoming;
Gift of Mr. and Mrs. Charles Belden; P.67.1.1.

Following the death of Louis Phelps in 1922, Charles and Eugene took over management of the Pitchfork. Charles and Frances would raise three children on the ranch, Margot, Annice and Mary Elizabeth, who died while quite young.

The Pitchfork Ranch and surrounding wilderness environments provided the ideal natural studio in which Charles could pursue his love of photography. Framed by Carter Mountain and the Greybull River Valley, he considered it to be a "photographer's paradise." Subject matter abounded in everyday surroundings, including cowboys and their horses, cattle, abundant wildlife and towering snow-capped peaks.

While conducting ranch work, Charles always carried his camera, a saddlebag full of glass negatives and a unipod in his rifle scabbard, keeping an ever-watchful eye for the perfect photograph. He even trained a favorite saddle horse to stand motionless until after the shutter clicked. His motto became, "If a picture does not tell a story, it is not worth taking."

And tell a story they did, as his photos became renowned for capturing Western life in that era. Having witnessed a classic moment, he might spend hours or days setting up a scene to capture every detail of the event, including lighting, background and both human and animal characters. At one time, he even trained a pet coyote to sit and howl upon command, using the wild canine in many classic photos such as the coyote howling on a hilltop silhouetted by a full moon. He further enhanced the scene or effect through his pioneering darkroom and printmaking procedures, including the application of sepia or silver-blue paint under low-light darkroom conditions. His ingenious techniques resulted in many of his most famous photographs, like Long Trail Winding and The Rescue, which are a study in contrast with dark figures against light backgrounds.

The late Jack Richard of Cody, a noted photographer in his own right, once told me he thought Charles Belden's sense of composition was the keenest he had ever seen. This artistic ability resulted in a distinctive style, which makes one pause and say, "That must be a Belden."

In addition to ranch life, Charles had an enduring interest in wildlife. Antelope had returned from the brink of

The Rescue
Cowboy Jack Rhodes, Sr. rescuing lost calf at Pitchfork Ranch.
Photo courtesy of Buffalo Bill Historical Center,
Cody, Wyoming; Gift of Mr. and Mrs. Charles Belden; P.67.5.1

extinction and were abundant on the Pitchfork, and Charles began capturing fawns and bottle raising them for transfer to zoos throughout the nation. His good friend Bill Monday, a renowned Western pilot, flew planeloads of antelope across the country. One shipment was flown to New York, loaded aboard the Hindenburg, and taken across the Atlantic to a German zoo. The big airship exploded and burned on a subsequent flight.

Belden and Bill Monday made some of the earliest aerial big game counts in Wyoming. The combination of Monday's flying ability and Belden's photographic talent allowed them to capture many herds on film for later tallying. Game managers of later years would use their data and emulate their census techniques.

Through time, Charles Belden's association with antelope and their conservation resulted in the nickname "Antelope Charley." He adopted a personal logo that was a stylized version of a buck antelope head, and was invited to give the inaugural address at the first One Shot Antelope Hunt.

Charles and Bill also conducted some of the earliest aerial fish planting in high-mountain lakes, dangerous flying to say the least. They also carried out one of the first wild horse roundups using an airplane.

Also a talented writer, Charles combined romantic Western prose with his stunning photographs to promote the dude ranch operation at the Pitchfork. A Belden photo on the cover of the February 1937 issue of *Life* magazine further enhanced the ranch's growing reputation. Among the guests he attracted were Amelia Earhart, Wallace Berry, Hope

Williams, Will Rogers and the Prince of Monaco.

Financial difficulties with the ranch and family discord became intolerable for Charles, and he left the Pitchfork Ranch in the early 1940s and relocated to Florida. His Wyoming associates felt Wyoming had suffered a great loss with his leaving. In addition to being a talented artist, he also was remembered as a Western gentleman of outstanding character. As his daughter, Margot, told me, "He was a fine man, always very kind and more than willing to help others."

While in Florida, he began touring and lecturing on photography. He toured for *National Geographic*, *Colliers*, and *The Saturday Evening Post* among others. Some of his travels took him to Europe, where Western enthusiasts flocked to hear him speak.

Charles' health began to fail during his late seventies, and he could no longer produce the writings and photographs which were so much a part of his persona. In 1966, he apparently took his own life.

The legacy of Charles Belden lives on through his photographs. He has preserved a wonderful era in Wyoming, one that could have been lost to history.

JAY LAWSON

Photo courtesy of the town of Dayton, Wyoming.

21

Hans Kleiber
Forest Ranger and Artist of the Big Horns

The stories of James Fenimore Cooper have flamed the imagination of young boys since the middle of the nineteenth century. When he published *The Deerslayer* in 1841, his mythic hero, Natty Bumppo, with his Kentucky rifle called "Killdeer," would actually motivate some young men to seek out wilderness adventures. Hans Kleiber was among them.

Hans Kleiber was born on August 24, 1887 while his parents were traveling in Germany. They soon returned to their home in northern Silesia, then part of the Austro-Hungarian Empire. Hans' father was a textile designer by trade, but his avocation was the study of natural history.

Hans Kleiber headed to Ranchester, Wyoming,
where he worked as a logger in the Big Horns.
He marked timber and hacked out railroad ties at Woodrock Camp.
In 1911, Hans received his official appointment as a forest ranger.
Photo courtesy of the town of Dayton, Wyoming.

Hans' grandfather and mother also shared this interest. His family would take long hikes in the Sudeten Mountains with Hans collecting and identifying plant and insect specimens. This interest in nature would last a lifetime.

Kleiber began sketching and painting with watercolor at a young age. His topics of choice were wild birds and nature scenes. In later years, he would write "They have been a part of my world since early boyhood."

Hans' parents also encouraged their son to read, with

During his early years as a Bighorn National Forest ranger,
Hans would spend weeks alone on patrol and inspection trips
to the northern Big Horns.
Photos and artwork courtesy of the town of Dayton, Wyoming.

his interest being drawn to books on exploration and
discovery. Returning from a trip to Vienna, his mother
presented him with a beautifully illustrated copy of James
Fenimore Cooper's *Leather Stocking Tales*. He was enthralled
with stories of romance and adventure such as *The Deerslayer*
and *The Last of the Mohicans*. He dreamed of the American
frontier and longed to see that far country.

Hans realized his dream when his family left Europe
in 1900 for a new home in Massachusetts. Though disappointed

Hans was designated ranger-at-large in 1920.
His new duties took him to the Washakie and Wind River country
where he did survey work of the Wind River glaciers.
This photo was taken by Sanford Mills
of the upper part of Knife Point Glacier.
It was published in *American Forests* magazine in 1922.
Photos and artwork courtesy of the town of Dayton, Wyoming.

in the manufacturing environment of New England, Hans was fortunate to study under artist and nature philosopher Clarence Blodgett. Clarence instructed Hans in the principles of art and also exposed him to the writings of Emerson and Thoreau as well as classical music.

Longing for the frontier, Hans became aware of President Theodore Roosevelt's plans to establish western forest reserves and a forest service, he resolved to head west. Arriving in Denver in 1906, he soon discovered that you had to be twenty-one years of age to enter the new Forest Service. Undeterred, he headed for Ranchester, Wyoming to work as a logger in the Big Horns. Arriving at a tie hack camp near Woodrock, he was soon put to work marking timber and hacking out railroad ties.

By the spring of 1908, Hans was old enough to become a Forest Ranger, and he took the first Ranger Examination given at Big Horn, Wyoming. Much of the exam was comprised of field exercises, including horse packing and judging timber. Hans had brought his guns along, but shooting proficiency was dropped at the last minute; he was disappointed, to say the least.

It wasn't until 1911 that Hans was able to get his citizenship papers in order and receive his official appointment as a Forest Ranger. In that same year, he returned to Massachusetts to marry Frances Millette.

Hans and Frances had two children, Rita and Stuart, but would eventually divorce in 1918 when Frances tired of the rugged frontier life in Wyoming. Hans' parents then moved west to Dayton, and his mother aided him in raising his small children.

Hans Kleiber sketching.
Photo courtesy of the town of Dayton, Wyoming.

Hans would spend weeks alone on horseback patrolling the northern Big Horns. Mountain solitude was his cup of tea, and he reveled in the wildness of his ranger district. His notes and sketches reflect a deep love of things natural.

Fire fighting was a major duty of early rangers, and Hans became proficient at organizing crews and directing their efforts on major fires. During one fire, Hans had worked for several days without sleep and decided to lie down behind a boulder to rest. A large burnt snag fell on the boulder and caused Hans some minor injuries, but he was able to limp back into camp.

Mallards in Flight.
Many of Hans Kleiber's etchings reflect
scenes he enjoyed while working in the Big Horn Mountains.
Artwork courtesy of the town of Dayton, Wyoming.

Crossing the Platte
reproduced by Hans Kleiber's son, Stuart.
Artwork courtesy of the town of Dayton, Wyoming.

Title Unknown
Artwork courtesy of the town of Dayton, Wyoming.

Hitching Rail
Artwork courtesy of the town of Dayton, Wyoming.

During the winter of 1915, Hans was asked to take over the Ten Sleep and Paintrock Ranger districts. He made the arduous journey on horseback in January, crossing between Tongue River and Shell Creek about where the highway goes now. The trip took four days in deep snow. Arriving at Hyattville, his overshoes were frozen into the stirrups and he had to be helped from his saddle.

In 1920, Hans Kleiber was designated a Ranger-at-Large, and his new duties took him to the Washakie and Wind River country. Following a survey of the Wind River glaciers, his notes on the geology and fauna of the area were published in *American Forests*.

Fishing was a favorite pastime, and the streams and high lakes of the Winder River range afforded Hans endless opportunities for angling. At times, he would carry a fishing rod, but if one was not available he always had a length of line with flies attached, wrapped around the brim of his hat, and would simply cut a willow branch and use it as an improvised fly rod.

Throughout his years as a forest ranger, Hans continued to sketch and draw, particularly scenes from nature. In 1923, he decided to leave the forest service, wishing to pursue a full-time art career—a bold move in those days.

He established a studio at his home near Dayton, Wyoming, and continued his work creating pen-and-ink drawings. This soon led to an interest in etchings, which involves engraving into a wax-covered plate and then rubbing ink into the engraved lines. The plate is then run through a printing press which can produce up to a hundred prints. Having little money and a family to support, Hans built his own printing press from scrap metal.

To supplement his income, Hans guided hunters in the fall; his knowledge of the Big Horn Mountains allowed him to access the best game country. One dude he met was Mr. Russell Kettell, an art connoisseur from Boston. Mr. Kettell took an instant liking to Hans and his artwork, offering to carry his prints back to the best art dealers in Massachusetts. The prints sold briskly in the East, and his reputation as a wilderness artist began to grow.

Hans Kleiber's art was soon in exhibitions at Goodspeed's, a well-known art dealer in Boston. Exhibitions around the country soon followed, and in 1929, Hans was awarded a silver medal by the International Printmakers of California for his etching, *Leaving the High Country*.

In 1931, Hans married Margaret Duff, from then on known as "Missy," and she would help him manage his art career in future years. A principle role for Missy was regulating the constant flow of visitors to their wilderness studio and ensuring that Hans had sufficient quiet time to draw and paint. She was also instrumental in promoting his work outside of Wyoming.

Hans had always enjoyed poetry and carried small editions of Lord Byron and Robert Burn's poems in his saddlebag during his ranger years. He, himself, also composed many poems during that time. After finding them years later in an old desk drawer, he had them published in 1963. Titled *Songs of the Big Horns*, their focus was on nature, much like his artwork.

His painting and etching continued until his vision began to fail during his late seventies. After passing away at the age of eighty, his wife, Missy, followed him in death six weeks later.

Kleiber's art continues to be enjoyed throughout the nation, and his short stories were published posthumously in a wonderful collection titled, *Daydreams and Fantasies—Stories of the Secret Forest.*

Hans Kleiber's log studio is now a small museum in the town of Dayton. Guests can view his handmade printing press, original Kleiber artwork, and the work of visiting artists.

Deputy game wardens James Spriggs (right)
and Fielding Peterson near Kemmerer
during the first successful antelope transplant in Wyoming.
Photo courtesy of Hazel Spriggs

22

James W. Spriggs
Restoring Wyoming's Wildlife

By the early 1930s, it was clear to Wyoming game wardens that protection alone would not recover many wildlife populations. When the smoke had cleared from decades of unregulated hunting and trapping, entire drainages were devoid of beaver, many mountain ranges were without elk, and deer were so scarce in some counties that a fresh track was the talk of the town.

In this dark hour for conservation, funding for the restoration of America's wildlife was provided by the Pittman-Robertson Act of 1937. Congress placed an excise tax on the sale of sporting arms and ammunition, thus allowing hunters to fund the re-establishment of wildlife populations across the nation.

A young James Spriggs and his family
return from a hunting trip above Dubois in 1918.
Their camp and the elk they harvested
were transported by horse-drawn wagon.
Photo courtesy of Hazel Spriggs.

Plans were laid in Wyoming to begin capturing and transplanting animals from areas of relatively high abundance. There wasn't much equipment and there were few techniques for capturing wildlife in those days, but there were highly skilled individuals in the game warden ranks who had grown up trapping wild animals and handling domestic stock. It was art more than science. These men really understood animal behavior and improvised methods to capture and handle wildlife. Special teams and survey crews were established for the species of greatest concern. One of the highest priorities was the re-establishment of beaver colonies. Game warden James Spriggs was chosen to lead that effort.

James Spriggs with a beaver.
Photo courtesy of Hazel Spriggs.

James Spriggs and three deputy game wardens
each release a beaver into new habitat
as part of the federal Pittman-Robertson wildlife restoration project.
Photo courtesy of Hazel Spriggs.

James Spriggs was born April 10, 1908, in Lander. As a young boy, he found Fremont County to be the perfect outdoor classroom. Though an excellent student and athlete, his first loves were hunting, fishing and studying wild birds and animals.

After graduating from high school in 1926, Jim drove the Yellowstone bus from Lander to Moran, taking tourists who had arrived by train to see the Park. It was an all-day trip, and he would sleep in a tent at Moran before making the return journey.

Warren Spriggs, son of James,
with a young beaver captured in a live trap.
Photo courtesy of Hazel Spriggs.

He enrolled in zoology at the University of Wyoming and soon became an outstanding athlete, competing on both the swimming and boxing teams. He won the Rocky Mountain welterweight championship.

In 1937, Jim married Hazel Hartman. They had two sons, Warren and Joe, and raised two children from Jim's previous marriage, Charlotte and Buddy.

Jim took the first game warden examination in 1938 and was hired because of his high scores. Given his skills in capturing animals, he soon was made team leader of the Pittman-Robertson beaver survey.

Following initial population inventories, Jim and his team began the live trapping of pairs of beaver and relocating them to areas where they had been extirpated. To enhance survival, he learned to withhold food from the beaver for twenty-four hours prior to transport. In addition, he found that placing them in a cage covered with wet canvas before moving them also reduced mortality. His techniques worked, and more than a thousand beaver were successfully relocated across the state, improving stream flows and fishing at the same time.

Jim was assigned to Afton in 1941, where he assisted with elk calf-tagging studies and transplanting elk. He also directed the establishment of the first elk feedground in Star Valley. During this period, Jim also began conducting range surveys to determine the availability of forage for big game before making decisions on the proper population size. This all was done on foot and horseback in the rugged Salt River and Wyoming ranges.

The first mule deer trapping project conducted near Greybull
on the west slope of the Big Horn Mountains.
These deer were transplanted to areas where the species
had virtually been eliminated.
Photo courtesy of Hazel Spriggs.

Antelope still were scarce in southwest Wyoming
in 1941, so Jim and fellow warden Fielding Peterson were
given the task of trapping antelope near Pathfinder Reservoir
and releasing them in the Kemmerer area as part of the
Pittman-Robertson project.

This antelope capture would be the first attempt to
use aircraft to drive antelope into a corral-type trap. Capturing
nearly seventy antelope in the first few days, the decision was
made to expand the effort, and antelope were moved to Big
Horn, Sublette and Uinta counties, where new herds
were established.

The next project for Jim was the trapping of deer on the west slope of the Big Horn Mountains. Instead of being driven, the deer were baited into the trap and were hauled by horse-drawn wagons to waiting trucks. The trucks carried the deer to eastern Wyoming to supplement dwindling herds. Jim made several modifications to his initial trap design and was able to capture several hundred deer.

When World War II broke out, Jim answered the call of duty and enlisted in the Marine Corps. At thirty-five, he was older than most Marines, but his outdoor life in Wyoming had made him extremely fit and he was an expert marksman. He would prove to be a formidable opponent for Japanese soldiers.

Trained to use both the rifle and flame-thrower, Jim would participate in major battles on Okinawa, Ryukyu, Guadacanal and other islands. One of the fortunate Marines to survive multiple landings, he was able to return to his family in Wyoming and resume his wildlife endeavors.

His first assignment upon returning from the service was to coordinate a statewide inventory of antelope. Single engine planes were rented for nine dollars per hour, and hundreds of hours were spent flying transects over occupied antelope habitat. Jim personally counted more than 48,000 antelope, and both wardens and sportsmen were ecstatic over the increase in antelope numbers. One plane crashed and was destroyed during the survey, but fortunately both the pilot and game warden survived.

Jim was assigned to the Dubois area in 1946 and was given the task of trapping bighorn sheep near Whiskey Mountain. Jim and Ned Frost had unsuccessfully attempted to trap bighorns on Jim Mountain west of Cody before the war, and he had learned from that experience.

This time, he constructed traps in open environments rather than timbered and used netting rather than panels. The changes worked, and he soon was shipping wild sheep to other mountain ranges.

In addition to his game warden duties, Jim trapped and shot over three hundred coyotes on bighorn sheep winter ranges in an effort to enhance lamb survival. Even the wily coyote was no match for his trapping skills.

After several years in Dubois, Jim's younger son Joe (named after artist Joe Back, who was featured earlier in this series) began having serious health problems. With no doctor in town, Jim and Hazel decided to relocate to Lander. Taking a leave of absence from the Game and Fish Department, Jim soon opened a small store and motel in Lander. Since he was involved in business, he did not return to a game warden position, though according to Hazel, his wildlife career had been "the highlight of his working life."

James W. Spriggs lived to age ninety-two, passing away July 5, 2000. He lived to see the fruits of his labors, as wildlife had recovered throughout Wyoming. As an index to the success of early restoration efforts, antelope harvest increased from fourteen hundred animals in 1935 to nearly ten thousand in 1946, and deer harvest went from eight hundred to thirteen thousand during the same period.

Today's hunters and wildlife enthusiasts owe a great deal to the old-time game wardens like James Spriggs. Their efforts, combined with hunter dollars and the Pittman-Robertson Act, have given us the wildlife we have today.

Photo courtesy of Wyoming Game and Fish Department.

23

Floyd Blunt
Rapport with the Wild

Once in a great while you find an individual with a natural gift for interacting with animals. It might be a cowboy, biologist, farmer or veterinarian—but those with real talent are rare. In the case of the Wyoming Game and Fish Department, Floyd Blunt was that person, and he came along at just the right moment in time.

Floyd Blunt was born in Hawk Springs, Wyoming, on January 24, 1916. His parents operated a ranch south of Guernsey at the mouth of Lone Tree Canyon, and his relationship with animals began during early boyhood. While still in elementary school, Floyd would rise in the dark,

Floyd was the first to develop techniques
that allowed many species to survive in captivity for research.
Floyd is feeding a bighorn lamb,
one of the more difficult species to maintain in a captive setting.
Photo courtesy of Wyoming Game and Fish Department.

harness a team of horses, and deliver milk for the neighboring dairy farm.

Floyd's abilities with animals became apparent when he handled horses with more success than most adults. He also had a small crossbred shepherd dog that he trained to work cattle. The dog was quite small and would tire on a long drive, so Floyd taught him to jump up behind the cantle of his saddle and ride on the horse's rump when he was not actually working cows.

Floyd graduated from Guernsey High School and went on to the University of Wyoming where he earned a degree in agricultural science. During his tenure at the university he worked several jobs to pay his way through school and still excelled academically. He could also be seen around campus flying a small falcon he had trained, often sending it up to catch a flying grasshopper or passing sparrow.

Floyd's interest in birds blossomed at the university, and he would eventually become one of the state's finest ornithologists. Fascinated by migration, he would band various species and record their arrival dates each spring.

Following graduation, Floyd joined the army to do his part in the second world war. He participated in the South Pacific campaign, and though he rarely spoke of his combat experience in the forests of New Guinea and elsewhere, his rise to master sergeant in a few short years speaks to his accomplishments.

Returning from the war, Floyd took the game warden examination and scored near the top. He was assigned to Saratoga, replacing Don Simpson, who had been shot and killed by a poacher.

It was not unusual for the Sybille Wildlife Research Unit
to do research on multiple species at any given time.
Here, Floyd is feeding a fawn deer while
an elk and moose calf wait their turn.
Photo courtesy of Wyoming Game and Fish Department.

Floyd's talents in the wildlife management field soon emerged, and he was encouraged to pursue an advanced degree at the University of Wyoming. Before he could complete his next degree he was called back to lead the department's wildlife restoration team.

Appointed Federal Aid Coordinator and Chief of the Wildlife Restoration Division in 1950, Floyd's work unit was soon trapping and transplanting wildlife around the state. His ability to handle wild animals under the most adverse conditions earned him quite a reputation during this era. Among his most notable accomplishments were the establishment of wild turkeys in the Black Hills and federal legislation enabling hunters to harvest elk in Grand Teton National Park for population control.

The department had obtained three thousand acres of land in Sybille Canyon for deer winter range during the 1940s, and Floyd felt this was the ideal location for a world class research facility he was convinced wildlife needed.

Floyd began visiting major zoos to study their operations, but soon realized that he would have to improvise a great deal, as actual research would necessitate regular handling of elk, bighorn sheep and other species. He also came to feel that handling techniques should not involve any harsh methods if wild animals were to adjust to a captive setting.

The design and construction of the new research facility began in 1952 under Floyd's direction, and he relocated to the unit in 1955 to supervise research efforts onsite. Studies were soon underway pertaining to parasites and disease in bighorn sheep, and elk nutrition, and mountain goats were evaluated for suitability in regard to transplants.

Declines in bighorn sheep populations
prompted years of research on this species,
much of it focused on parasites and disease.
Photo courtesy of Wyoming Game and FishDepartment.

A deer fawn waits anxiously
as Floyd prepares the formula for the day's feeding.
Photo courtesy of Wyoming Game and Fish Department.

Sybille was the first of its kind, and Floyd had to design chutes and pens for animal handling. Many of his innovations would be copied in later years by zoos and research facilities. Floyd led by example, encouraging every researcher to emulate his calm demeanor, steady voice and slow, deliberate actions to avoid exciting captive wildlife. His philosophy was to "let the animal figure out what you wanted." I first met Floyd in the late 1970s when I delivered a calf elk to Sybille, and his unique personality and calming influence on animals was amazing to me. He made an indelible impression.

When asked about his ability to quiet animals and handle them, Floyd said you had to develop "simpatico," or mutual interaction and understanding that allowed you to gain their confidence.

There were many challenges in the early years, as many species had never survived captivity elsewhere. Floyd was the first person to raise moose successfully, and his dietary experiments led to the use of unique foods such as sugar beets and citrus pulp, combined with native browse.

Initially, many fawn antelope at Sybille suffered from digestive problems, but after studying free-ranging pronghorn mothers interacting with their young, Floyd implemented a bottle-feeding routine that included five daily feedings and the inducement of defecation through the use of a warm, moist towel massaged over their rump; the problems disappeared.

Rather than herd animals towards handling pens, Floyd developed a large wooden barrier with slits he could see through, and would slowly move animals to desired locations without exciting them.

Even among wild critters there is variation in

personality and behavior, and several animals and birds stick out when you think of Floyd's time at Sybille. For example, the bull moose pictured in this article had been bottle-raised and did not fear humans; he was aggressive towards others, but would allow Floyd to draw blood from him without restraint.

An injured great horned owl that Floyd rehabilitated was quite a character. Since it was a juvenile bird, Floyd decided to do a "soft" release back to the wild—meaning that he would provide some food for a short while until the owl began hunting on its own. Each evening he would imitate an owl's call, and soon the bird would answer him and come flying in for his food. On several days Floyd was late for this ritual and the owl would land on the office windowsill and bang his beak against the glass.

One cow elk, nicknamed Susie, was a fixture at Sybille for eighteen years. Part of a transplant from Yellowstone to Laramie Peak, she had been injured in transport, and rancher Owen McGill placed the little calf in his barn until he could haul her to Sybille and Floyd's care. She carried a scar on her back that set her apart and became so in tune with Floyd that he could experiment with new collar designs or take samples from her without even using a chute.

In 1967, the department hired its first wildlife veterinarian, Tom Thorne. He and Floyd became fast friends, and their combined expertise allowed them to conduct pioneering research on the diseases afflicting Wyoming's wildlife.

After nearly thirty years of research, Floyd Blunt retired in 1980, and built a home in Sybille Canyon not far upstream from the unit. He continued his study of birds and also offered to rehabilitate birds and small mammals for the department.

One spring day I was about to leave the regional Game and Fish office in Laramie when a distraught woman pulled up and told me she had accidentally run over a hen mallard that was leading her brood across a city street. I followed her to the site and eventually gathered up all the downy ducklings and placed them in a carrier. I then called Floyd, who told me to bring them to his house in the canyon.

When I arrived, Floyd ran some lukewarm water into a metal tub, placed the ducklings in it, and we then went up the hill behind his house and selected several flat rocks that would allow them to rest and preen just above the water level. Floyd and I visited as he began cooking some hard-boiled eggs and making a concoction to feed the young birds. All the while, a magpie and a Clark's nutcracker, each with a band on its leg, perched on the edge of the porch and watched this operation. When it came time for me to leave, there was a beautiful Say's phoebe in my vehicle, so we opened the doors and had a good laugh while we waited for it to fly out.

I returned to visit Floyd that fall. As I drove into his yard, the mallards, now grown up, were flying around his house and landing in his manmade pond. These ducks would later migrate south. I have always felt that Floyd's willingness to help those birds when he was quite elderly exemplified his lifelong devotion to wild creatures.

Floyd Blunt passed away on October 25, 1997, and though unaware, Wyoming's wildlife suffered a huge loss on that day. Huey Dawson, Floyd's good friend and successor at

Photo courtesy of Wyoming Game and Fish Department.

Sybille, followed his wishes and sprinkled Floyd's ashes among the animals at the research unit.

Perhaps biologist and researcher Bill Hepworth summed up Floyd Blunt best when he said, "He was a friend to man and animal alike."

And when I think of Floyd living and working for decades along the road in Sybille Canyon, his relationships with humans bring to mind the final verse of his favorite poem, Sam Walter Foss's, *The House by the Side of the Road.*

> *Let me live in my house by the side of the road*
> *Where the race of men go by;*
> *They are good, they are bad, they are weak,*
> *They are strong,*
> *Wise, foolish—so am I.*
> *Then why should I sit in the scorner's seat*
> *Or hurl the cynic's ban?*
> *Let me live in my house by the side of the road*
> *And be a friend to man.*

His relationship with animals evokes Rudyard Kipling's description of King Solomon's mythical ability to communicate with beasts and birds.

> *There was never a king like Solomon*
> *Not since the world began*
> *Yet Solomon talked to a butterfly*
> *As a man would talk to a man.*

Leone rests on the bull elk
taken by her son-in-law, Kenny Pickinpaugh, in 1999.
Photo courtesy of Leone Olds.

24

Leone Olds
The French Trapper's Daughter

A few years back, I was visiting with game warden Joe Gilbert about some of the colorful characters we have encountered out in the hills. He told me about checking elk hunters in the Laramie Range and coming upon a woman who had just killed a bull elk while hunting alone; she was preparing to pack it out on her back.

Joe's story caught my interest, but when he added the fact she was hunting in a snowstorm and wearing a long skirt and a cowboy hat, I knew I had to meet this woman. Her name was Leone Olds, and he thought she lived near Douglas.

When I began writing this series, Leone's name was on

my list of folks to contact; this past month I was lucky enough to meet her and have a fascinating visit about the intriguing life she has led in central Wyoming.

Leone's father, Leon Beaulieu, immigrated to Wyoming from Quebec, Canada, in around 1890. Leon, still in

Illustration by Brian Maebius.

his early teens, could only speak French, which made communication difficult; however, being a hard worker, he was soon employed by area ranchers.

In 1896, Leon homesteaded on Crazy Horse Creek. He built a cabin, barn and chicken coop out of logs. He then bought a wood-burning stove and some of the chairs from the Douglas Opera House. This was the beginning of his ranch.

An accomplished trapper, Leon was known locally as "The French Trapper" or "The French Wolfer." His specialty was wolves, which carried a bounty at that time, and he set a personal goal of catching one hundred in a winter season. Although he never achieved that number, he managed to catch ninety-nine in one year, for which he was held in high regard by local ranchers.

Leon Beaulieu married Gata McCarthy, the Cold Springs school teacher (she had one pupil at the time) in 1931. One year later, Gata gave birth to a daughter, Gata Leone Beaulieu. With both her father and mother as namesakes, she would go by "Leone," a female variation of the French male name Leon. Making a living in the mountains could be a struggle, but the enterprising Leon managed to support his new family by trapping, sheep ranching and prospecting.

Leone's earliest recollection of wildlife occurred when she was only two or three years old. Leone's father had left her with a small drop herd of sheep, as the dog they were using would not stay with the flock unless a person was present. Sitting in the grass while the dog was on the other side of the sheep, a coyote approached her. Being quite small, she was actually looking up at the coyote when the dog returned and

Like hunting and trapping, Leone learned to fish at an early age.
"The French Trapper," Leon Beaulieu,
and daughter, Leone, display their dinner in 1944.
Photo courtesy of Leone Olds.

ran it off. Even at that young age, she resolved to always
have a means of protecting herself, even if it was only a good
stout stick.

A neighboring rancher, Melvin Stinson, took an
interest in teaching Leone outdoor skills and taught her to
shoot a .22 rifle at an early age—maybe six or seven—she was
a natural shot. Her rifle had a slight bend in the barrel, which
made for tricky shooting, but she eventually learned to

compensate and rarely missed a target.

At the age of nine, Leone's father sent her out to hunt a deer, as they were out of meat. He gave her a 7x57 Mauser rifle he had brought back from World War I and one cartridge. Sneaking through the forest, Leone came across a nice mule deer buck, and she shot him through the heart. Her father did not feel she was old enough to carry a sharp knife, so she ran all the way back to the ranch to get him and bring him back to field dress the deer and pack it out by horse and wagon.

Leone ran her own trap line from the age of twelve, and that experience taught her much about the habits of wildlife. She learned to decipher tracks and other sign, fostering a lifelong interest in animal behavior. The furs she and her father sold provided additional income for the ranch.

At sixteen, Leone married Ralph Olds. Although Ralph was not a hunter, he appreciated the fact that his new wife was, and he enjoyed the wild meat she provided.

Mule deer had declined in numbers in the Laramie Range, but the elk that had been transplanted and restored to those mountains were growing in abundance. Leone decided to "quit the deer" and concentrate on elk.

Hunting with a trusted old 30-30 lever action rifle, Leone would hunt elk alone, learning to stalk within close range to make a single killing shot. In the early years she would shoot calves, often packing them out one half at a time. Later on she shot a few cows and packed the individual quarters out. Then one year she shot a 5-point bull, which produced a large amount of excellent meat. From then on she was "after the bulls."

By hunting alone, Leone could move slowly and quietly through forest habitats, just the way she learned to do as a child. One fall she was sneaking up on a big bull bedded under the face of a large granite outcrop. As she crept up the back side of the formation, she spooked a coyote. Its only escape was to run directly at Leone, and it actually ran to the edge of her skirt before panicking and heading back up the ledge, eventually tripping over a branch and tumbling over the edge.

Leone Olds and grandson, Brady Vollman, pose with their trophies.
Photo courtesy of Leone Olds.

Suddenly there was a big commotion, as the coyote had landed on top of the elk. The bull ran out and stopped to look back, but in all the excitement Leone missed the shot.

Leone has a very fair complexion, and she used to wear heavy pancake makeup as a form of sunscreen. Many early forms of makeup had animal oils as a base, and at times Leone would have wild critters approach her as she was sitting or making a stand—apparently attracted by the scent of the cosmetic.

Her husband Ralph passed away in 1994, and Leone continued to run several small businesses they created together. She also continued hunting.

During the fall of 1998, at the age of sixty-six, Leone was making a stand by a mountain pass where she knew elk frequently traveled. As she was waiting in ambush, an elk herd appeared about two miles away, consisting of several spikes, some cows and calves, and a huge bull. Leone thought, "I want one of the spikes."

As the elk approached, it became apparent they were headed toward the next pass to the west; she decided to move and conceal herself at that location. Suddenly, the big bull appeared by himself, and Leone dropped him with a single shot. While field dressing her trophy, she discovered he had been grazed in the brisket by a bullet, which may explain his splitting off from the herd. He was a monster, later scoring more than 349 Boone and Crocket points.

Although Leone normally packed elk out on her back, she decided to return with a fellow rancher and a big horse to retrieve the old bull. As it was very rugged and remote terrain, it took them all day to get the job done.

Leone and her women friends
are known to occasionally wet their lines.
The stringer of fish Leone is holding is an example
of their success in 1997.
Photo courtesy of Leone Olds.

This past fall Leone hunted by herself for nearly thirty days, often hunting on her original family homestead and ranch, which she still owns. She shot a spike bull for her winter's meat and enjoyed every minute of the outing. And yes, she was hunting in her usual outdoor attire—a long skirt and a cowboy hat or scarf.

Each year, I have a number of men in their fifties or early sixties tell me they are giving up elk hunting as it is just too physically demanding. Now when I hear that lament, I can't help but think of Leone Olds, stalking bull elk at the age of seventy-three! Perhaps we guys should consider keeping in shape and staying in the hills for one more season.

As they say, "Cowboy up."

Photo courtesy of Wyoming Game and Fish Department.

25

Snook Moore
Life as Wilderness Adventure

During the early twentieth century, there were still a handful of rugged individuals spending their entire lives in the wilderness; making a living from the land in various ways, not wanting to "move to town" or leave the high country. One of the most classic examples is Snook Moore.

Arthur Earl "Snook" Moore was born in Pinedale, Wyoming, on February 12, 1916. The town was young and the country still wild, and Snook took to that environment like a natural.

His connection with horses started at the age of four, when his father took him on a thirty-mile ride. When he was twelve, Snook broke his first horse, and by sixteen he was wrangling for the DC Bar Ranch and rodeoing on Sundays.

Hunting and fishing were part of everyday life, and Snook was soon proficient at both—always eager to supply a grouse for the pot or provide a stringer of fresh trout for supper. He trapped for spending money, as fur prices remained fairly high even during the Depression; a marten bringing close to twenty dollars, a mink being worth a week's pay.

When he turned eighteen, Snook went to work for the Green River Cattle Association. He was appointed the rough-string rider and given nine half-broke "outlaws" to put the finish on. The association had twelve thousand head of cattle on a one hundred square mile mountain pasture, so there were many big circles to ride. In addition, Snook had become a proficient farrier, and many evenings were spent trimming and shoeing horses for the outfit's cowboys.

Snook met his future wife, Evalyn, during a dance at the DC Bar. She had come to Wyoming from California to teach at the remote Kendall School and was taken with the handsome young cowboy. They were married on August 12, 1939. Wanting to live in the mountains, Snook and Evalyn acquired a quarter section of land right where Tosi and Tepee Creeks converge in the upper Green River drainage. It had been homesteaded by pioneer Bert Westland and later acquired by Snook's great uncle, Dan Doyle. The price was a thousand dollars, a big sum in those days.

Forty miles from any settlement, and with only a sod-roofed one-room cabin, the little ranch was one of the most remote in the state. In addition, that country is snowed in from November through April. The first winter was an

Snook drives his draft-horse team and wagon in the beautiful Green River Valley.
Snook used the team to cut and move his hay and to feed his other stock during the winter.
Photo courtesy of Wyoming Game and Fish Department.

Snook and Evalyn stand in front of their cabin
just after the main lodge had been lost in a fire,
which consumed all of their possessions.
Photo courtesy of Wyoming Game and Fish Department.

adventure, but they vowed to stick it out, even though some folks thought they were crazy.

During the first few summers, Snook cleared sagebrush and created a grass hay meadow. He then began building several cabins. Using an ax and a one-man crosscut saw, he would fell trees and skid them into place with his saddle horse. Many locals wondered what a cowboy knew about building cabins, but he got the job done.

To pay off his ranch, Snook would cowboy all summer and then run a fifty-mile trapline on snowshoes during the long winter. The pelts of pine marten, beaver, coyotes and other furbearers soon allowed him to settle his debt. As with many of his outdoor talents, Snook was soon held in high regard for his ability to properly prepare furs; his perfectly fleshed and stretched hides always brought top dollar.

Through time, Snook developed an intimate knowledge of the wilderness surrounding his ranch, and he decided to go into the outfitting business. He acquired a good string of horses, many of them crossbred Arabian-Quarter horses—they were his favorites—with a smooth and fast gait and plenty of endurance. He also obtained a pair of draft horses to cut and haul his hay and help feed his other stock by wagon in the winter.

During the summer, Snook would pack guests up the Roaring Fork to numerous lakes, many near or above timberline. It is stunning country, and years later many former guests would proclaim those fishing trips were the finest adventures they had experienced in a lifetime. His knowledge of the high country was unique, and since the Wyoming Game and Fish Department was attempting to stock trout in dozens of subalpine lakes in the northern portion of the Wind River Range, they contracted with Snook to pack in milk cans full of fish. In some cases, he would haul the milk cans himself if he was unable to get a horse to the lakeshore.

Sheep hunting was Snook's forte, and his ability to find trophy rams for his clients became legend. But they had to earn those trophies, as Snook hunted some of the most rugged terrain in all of western Wyoming. One incident illustrates just how fit and physically tough he was in those years. He had packed a sheep hunter into the country above Green River Lakes, and they had left their horses in a blind canyon, forming a natural corral with a few logs Snook had stashed there to construct a gate or barrier. They then took backpacks and climbed toward the top of the Wind River Range. As they approached the divide, the hunter began having chest pains and collapsed, apparently from a heart attack.

Snook knew time was of the essence, so he slung the man over his shoulder and dropped into the Tourist Creek drainage, a maze of giant boulders and avalanche chutes. Dropping several thousand feet in elevation while carrying a grown man, he reached the horses in only a few hours. The victim was not conscious enough to ride, so Snook draped him over the saddle and headed down country. At the head of the lower lake, someone had left a boat, so Snook placed the hunter in it and rowed across to a dude ranch, which was located where the campground is today. From there, an ambulance was summoned. Miraculously, the man survived.

Snook loved to hunt elk in the Gros Ventre drainage

Part of Snook's string of packhorses was kept in the corral.
Every cabin and corral was hand-built by Snook
with logs he cut in the nearby forest.
Photo courtesy of Wyoming Game and Fish Department.

and the Sportsman Ridge country, but it was a long pack back to the ranch. To save hunting time, he would often load several packhorses with elk meat, take them to the divide, and then send them home on their own. Evalyn would find the horses standing at the gate, and she would unpack the elk meat and put them in the corral. Fritz Yenko of Rock Springs used to hunt that same country, and told me of his amazement when several pack horses loaded with meat passed him on the trail.

Hunting trips should be adventures in Snook's mind, and at times he would take antelope hunters out on horseback, hunting a few old bucks that stayed up high in the Gros Ventre Range rather than shooting one with ease in the low country.

Through time, Snook collected several fabulous trophies, and he learned taxidermy through a correspondence course so he could mount them himself. His best sheep was a fifteen year old ram that game warden Duke Early says was one of the biggest to come out of those mountains. He shot a 7-point bull elk with nearly a five-foot inside spread, a record-book moose and several huge mule deer bucks. Nearly every trophy was taken with a 30-30 Winchester carbine at close range.

One year, a grizzly bear moved into the head of Tosi Creek just above the Moore Ranch. Evalyn decided to accompany Snook when he hunted the big bear. Near the divide, they encountered the grizzly, a huge male who stood up at the sight of them. The bear charged and Snook hit him four times with his old saddle gun, the bear literally falling at his feet. He sent the bear's hide to a tannery and then made a rug from it, which they hung over the fireplace.

In the early 1950s, Snook began feeding elk below Green River Lakes for the Game and Fish. It was twenty-four miles round trip on skis, snowshoes or with his dog team, and he made that daily trek all winter for nineteen years. One can only imagine the endurance required of both him and his dogs.

In 1979, Snook and Evalyn lost their main cabin and hunting lodge to a fire. Nearly everything was destroyed— the huge bighorn ram and elk heads, a record-size mounted cutthroat trout, the grizzly bear rug, photographs and memorabilia from the wilderness and all of their handmade furnishings went up in flames as they stood and watched, listening to the canned goods exploding inside.

The fire was a huge setback, but they never lost their natural optimism or good nature. Snook and Evalyn stayed on, still doing some outfitting and hosting numerous guests who had become close friends over the years. Snook continued to hunt, shooting an elk, deer and antelope each year and canning the meat for winter provisions.

In 1982, at the age of sixty-six, Snook was removing a hayrack when his horses spooked and ran away with his bobsled. Both runners ran over him and he was badly hurt. Evalyn was not home, so he caught the team, led them to the barn, unharnessed both horses and turned them out. He then saddled a dependable riding horse and headed down the valley. His favorite dog, Moose, a big Chesapeake cross who functioned as a sled dog and retrieved shot beavers, knew something was wrong and came with him.

Two forest service employees encountered Snook and could see he was injured, so one drove him to the Circle S Ranch while the other one rode his horse in. Snook was more worried about his animals than himself, and a ranch hand offered to take his horse and dog back to the ranch and feed the cows, horses and chickens. Taken to the hospital in Jackson, Snook was diagnosed with broken shoulders, seven broken ribs and internal injuries. Six weeks later he was back working at the ranch.

As Snook approached eighty, he slowed down somewhat, but he and Evalyn continued to live their austere

They were totally self-sufficient,
eating mostly wild game and keeping a flock of chickens
to produce what eggs they needed.
Photo courtesy of Wyoming Game and Fish Department.

wilderness life—no electricity, plumbing or telephone, and heating with a woodstove when temperatures commonly hovered below zero. Concerned neighbors brought over an older snowmobile as a safety measure in case he or Evalyn needed to get to town, but when they started it to make sure it would run, the throttle stuck, and it made a big circle and came right back at them. That convinced Snook that such contraptions weren't for him!

Several young men adopted Snook as their mentor, learning the ways of the mountains. Todd Stearns of Pinedale became one of his closest friends and took over elk feeding on the Upper Green. Like Snook, he spends the majority of every year in the wilderness.

Even in his last years, Snook continued to travel on snowshoes, securing firewood or just seeing what was going on in the country. Rancher Stan Murdock told me that Snook would occasionally find a cow that had become rimrocked or trapped by ice and missed during the Green River Cattlemen's fall roundup. Snook would break trail for the animal or get some feed to it, and then send word down the valley so the cowboys could come up and get their missing stock before winter really set in. He was helpful to both man and animal right to the end.

Snook Moore passed away at his beloved ranch on October 31, 1996. Evalyn would eventually move to town and follow him in death shortly after. Snook had cowboyed off and on for sixty years, fed elk for twenty years, and guided sheep hunters for forty-three years. His passing was truly the end of an era.

Photo courtesy of National Cowgirl Museum and Hall of Fame.

26

Brida Gafford
Wyoming's World Champion Cowgirl

During the early 1970s, an elderly woman was often seen riding her horse or driving an old pickup into Edgerton, Wyoming. Some of the younger kids jokingly referred to her as "Cactus Kate," as she lived alone on a remote ranch near the base of Pine Ridge at the Converse/Natrona county line. Her name was Brida Gafford, and only a few folks knew of her fascinating life.

Brida Gafford was born on June 4, 1896 in LaCross, Wisconsin. Extremely precocious and self-confident, she reportedly began riding horses when only two years old. Brida and horses would be a natural combination for life.

Sent to live with her grandparents before she was ten years old, she and her grandmother were often at odds due to her wild nature and strong personality. Brida ran away several times—threatening to join the circus as a girl trick rider. Finally, while still in grade school, Brida took the money she was given for school clothes and bought a train ticket to Miles City, Montana. She had heard tales of the Western life, and figured that was the place to become a real cowgirl.

Stranded at the train station in Miles City with no money left and only the clothes on her back, she was discovered by a local couple, the Turners, who kindly took her home to live with them. Word soon got around that the young girl had tremendous riding ability, and a stock promoter named Billy Richardson recruited her to ride in flat races, which she was soon winning.

Women rode saddle broncs in that era, and Brida Gafford had an uncanny ability to stick on the roughest broncs, often laughing as the horse tried in vain to buck her off. She entered her first rodeo in 1910, at the tender age of fourteen. Considered a child protégé, her success was resented by some of the older competitors.

Married at seventeen to a man named Henry Shimek, Brida moved to his farm in Nebraska. Henry died a few years later during the 1918 flu epidemic. Brida tried to make a go of it on the farm but was soon forced to sell out.

Looking for work, Brida heard about the oil boom at Midwest, Wyoming, and showed up there in 1921. She worked as a boarding house cook for a time but wanderlust got the best of her and she bought a saddle horse and pack horse and headed cross-country for the Cody Stampede.

A young Brida Gafford poses in trick riding regalia.
This must have been one of her first championship saddles.
A crack shot—she carries her pistol in her right hand
and a headless sage grouse in her left.
Notice her silhouette on the horse's neck.
Photo courtesy of National Cowgirl Museum and Hall of Fame.

Her rodeo experience at Cody reignited her desire to compete-so she rode on up to Montana for several events, then back to Cheyenne, and on down to Colorado. She would either sleep on the ground or stop at ranch houses, often doing a few days work for her keep. As her success grew, she could afford to take the train to big events in the Midwest and the east coast.

Brida Gafford makes a winning ride on "Suicide"
during the Pendleton Round-Up, 1927.
Photo courtesy of National Cowgirl Museum and Hall of Fame.

Even though she had been dragged around by a big
bronc in Chicago and suffered internal injujries, Brida decided
to join Miller's 101 Wild West and Far East Show. But her
injuries soon caught up with her and she nearly died on an
operating table. Determined to return to Wyoming, she
insisted they put her on a stretcher in a sleeper train and
headed to Douglas.

Following her recuperation, Brida homesteaded at a remote site near Pine Ridge in 1925. She would live there for decades—no electricity, no plumbing, no running water. Almost totally self-sufficient, she raised a garden, hunted, made her own clothes and broke horses for herself and others.

In 1926, she married rodeo cowboy Roy Gafford. Although they would stay married for years, he was often gone for long periods and Brida had to run the place on her own. Although she loved ranch life, her early success on the rodeo circuit had given her a taste for the big time and as she was completely healed up now—rodeo began calling and she knew she must go.

Traveling to Madison Square Garden in 1928, Brida won her first World Championship. She returned each year until 1937, winning on three occasions. She would also take the championship bronc riding contest in Cheyenne.

Trick riding was in big demand, and Brida taught a horse named "Whiskey" to leap over a convertible with the top down. Rancher Billie Beaton of Midwest, a well-known horsewoman herself, remembers watching Brida practicing "Roman Jumping" at the Salt Creek rodeo grounds. This involved standing on the saddles of two matched pintos as they jumped over a car. Brida developed quite a reputation and as Billie put it, "I heard of her long before I met her."

Following her rodeo career, Brida returned to her remote homestead. She and Roy ran a small bunch of cows and supplemented their income by trapping bobcats and coyotes. Brida's barn often had a number of pelts tacked to it.

Brida almost met her demise during the winter of 1949. Beginning in early January, a series of vicious blizzards

Brida riding a saddle bronc in Chicago.
She would later be badly injured during a ride in that city.
Photo courtesy of National Cowgirl Museum and Hall of Fame.

dropped more than one hundred inches of snow in some places. Literally buried in snow at her ranch, Brida melted snow for water and shot jackrabbits with her pistol when they came after her last remnant of hay. Her rugged and determined character allowed her to survive.

In her late years, many folks would seek Brida out for advice on horses and horse training. My good friend Wade Fraley was living in Edgerton in the early 1960s. He and some friends captured a small herd of wild horses. They planned to green break them and take them to the sale ring but the horses were covered with lice and had lost most of their hair. Brida came over, took one look and started building a big fire. She filled the bottom half of a barrel with water and brought it to a boil. She then sent Wade to the mercantile to purchase five or six plugs of tobacco, which she threw in the barrel. She then took an old insecticide sprayer, filled it with the concoction and sprayed down the horses. Within days, the lice were dead and the mustangs were growing shiny new coats.

Brida Gafford died in the spring of 1978, riding the horses she loved right up to the end. Like many of the colorful characters in these stories, her life is now little known. Hopefully this story will revive the fascinating history of one of Wyoming's greatest cowgirls.

Henry started guiding in 1914;
he and Frances outfitted from 1943 to 1975.
Photo courtesy of the Purvis Family.

27

Henry and Frances Purvis
Dwellers of the Thorofare

Perhaps nothing can bring a couple closer together than a mutual love of the outdoors. This was surely the case with Henry and Frances Purvis of Cody, Wyoming. When they married in 1917, the *Northern Wyoming Herald* reported, "Next-to-Nature Wedding of Popular South Fork Lovers."

Henry was on leave from the Army's Rainbow Division and about to ship out for World War I. The couple decided to marry before he left for war, and planned an evening wedding at the home of the bride's parents, Mr. and Mrs. M.L. Jones of Ishawooa. Unable to locate a minister at that late hour, they woke the justice of the peace near

Frances Purvis hangs out the wash to dry in the upper Thorofare.
Photo courtesy of the Purvis Family.

midnight and were married by lantern light on the banks of the South Fork of the Shoshone River. A perfect beginning for two outdoor lovers.

The families of both Henry and Frances had come to the Cody country in the early years. Henry was born in Cambridge, Nebraska on March 13, 1893. His family moved to Cody when he was two years old. They settled on Owl Creek near Thermopolis, but when Henry's mother died in 1900, his father left him, his four brothers and his sister with other families and moved back to Nebraska.

Henry literally raised himself, working for the famous Rocky Mountain Cattle Company as a cowboy at the age of eleven. He then worked for Colonel William F. "Buffalo Bill" Cody at the TE Ranch. Henry would recall the Colonel as a very congenial employer who always tried to eat with his cowboys. At that time, Col. Cody was riding a pony that would pretend to be lame so the Colonel would take him home. Cody's generosity "broke him," according to Henry, and when he was forced to sell off some of his stock, he gave Henry the choice of any horse in his string prior to the auction.

Like Henry, Frances also just missed becoming a native, as her mother was visiting in Montana when she was

Frances guides a successful elk hunter during the 1940s.
Her artificial leg did not deter her in the mountains.
Photo courtesy of the Purvis Family.

born in 1900. Growing up at Ishawooa, Frances literally grew up on horseback; horses and riding became a lifelong passion.

Henry served in the infantry and cavalry for two years during World War I. At about the time he returned, Frances developed a blood clot in her leg. Fearing gangrene, the doctor amputated the leg approximately four inches below the knee. Fitted with a wooden prosthesis, she was soon back on horseback—becoming so adept that she could even catch wild horses, one of the ultimate tests of a rider's skill.

The Purvises had three children, Paul, Frank and Grace. Both Paul and Frank would fly bombing missions during World War II, and Paul received two distinguished Flying Crosses for his heroic actions as a B-17 copilot.

Hunting guide Doug Hunter packs a trophy ram head
over an elk head as they prepare to head out of the Thorofare.
Photo courtesy of Doug Hunter.

Henry worked at various jobs during the 1920s and 1930s, but in 1943 he and Frances decided to go into the outfitting business full-time. With their mutual love of horses and hunting, they were well suited to the rigors of guiding in the high country. They founded a camp on Bruin Creek in the Thorofare, which had a great spring and abundant game in all directions.

In the early years, hunts would often last thirty days, but eventually they established ten-day hunts for four to five hunters. Doug and Warren Hunter guided for the Purvises in the 1950s and 1960s. They told me that prior to the beginning of the elk season, they would gather the horses at Henry's place and herd them upriver to the wilderness trailhead. As Doug put it, "If they bucked, they were pack horses; if they didn't, they were saddle horses." In those years, there was no regulation regarding tying horses head-to-tail, so there are great old photos of the big pack string lined out with full loads and headed into the Thorofare.

There were many colorful characters who stopped by the Bruin Creek camp. Son Paul related to me how guide and wrangler Frankie Lasiter would often drop in for a cup of coffee. Running the pack string from Valley Ranch, Frankie always walked and led his horses the thirty miles into the Thorofare. He always wore tennis shoes and, since the hiking kept him warm, a minimal amount of clothing. One cold and rainy day, he stopped by and was literally half frozen. Putting him close to the cook stove to thaw out, Henry had to demand that he accept warm boots and a coat before heading on his way.

Nettie Borner worked for the Purvis camp for years.

She would later start her own hunting camp on Younts Creek and it is now known on the maps as Borner Meadow.

In later years, the Purvis camp moved to Woody Creek. It was a high elevation camp made possible by a small but dependable spring. The advantage of being that high was the accessibility to game, with elk and sheep often taken just above camp. They would adorn the wall tents with elk antlers and the photos depict a high success rate. Those were wonderful times.

Henry and Frances were still in the Thorofare during the early 1970s. Retired Cody Game Warden Dave Bragonier encountered them on horseback at Bridger Lake in 1971; Henry was seventy-eight, Frances seventy-one. It is hard to

The Purvis packstring heads down the Deer Creek trail.
Photo courtesy of Doug Hunter.

imagine how many times they had made that arduous journey, particularly with Frances's artificial leg, but they were having a grand time riding through their old haunts. When Dave asked Henry how many years he had hunted the Thorofare, he reached into his pocket and produced his 1914 hunting license.

Henry passed away in 1985, and Frances followed him in 2000. They are still remembered fondly as the "Popular South Fork Lovers."

JAY LAWSON

In Conclusion

Just two weeks after finishing this book I was fly fishing on the North Fork of the Shoshone River west of Cody, an area where many of these stories took place. The country is still big and beautiful, and the river murmurs to you as it did to the old-timers. Sitting on a rock at the river's edge, I could picture in my mind's eye the adventures that took place at that very location.

You can travel upriver a few miles to the mouth of Green Creek and envision the original Frost and Richards ranchhouse with its seventeen rooms and a corral filled with fine horses. Many great adventures had their start from that lavish setting. The twentieth century's most famous archers, including Howard Hill, Dr. Saxton Pope and Art Young, would set off into the hills from there.

Going further upriver, Buffalo Bill Cody guided the Prince of Monaco from a North Fork camp that became known as "Camp Monaco" after Royal Artist, Louis Tinayre, carved the camp's name along with a bear paw print into a section of an ancient Englemann spruce tree.

Looking southwest toward Wapiti Ridge, you can form a mental image of Max Wilde breaking out on top with a big string of horses. And you can think of how this country inspired such romantic place names—Seclusion Creek, Fishhawk Creek, Cougar Creek, Glacier Basin, Petrified Ridge, Hawk's Rest, and Ishawooa Creek, where Anson Eddy is buried near the cabin site at which he spent decades with his horses and cats.

If you go south around Sheep Mountain to the South Fork, there will be the Purvis place, where you can imagine the guides herding horses upriver for the start of another splendid fall in the high country.

Up above Valley Ranch, you think about all the wonderful horses that have been in these mountains and the thousands of bull elk they have packed out on the long, rugged thirty-mile trek from the Thorofare Wilderness to the trailheads at Deer Creek and Ishawooa.

And today, I would rather sit on the banks of the Shoshone and reflect back on all the men, women and horses that created those adventures than catch the biggest trout in the river.

So it is with Wyoming—everywhere you go there are great stories, many of which are silently fading away. My purpose in writing this book was to preserve a small part of our history; I hope you feel I have achieved that goal.

My further hope is that these stories will encourage parents to ensure young people are exposed to the intrinsic qualities of Wyoming, its mountains, prairies, and wildlife. In this fast-paced age of electronic attachment, many children experience little adventure outside of virtual reality games—when, in fact, the real adventures lie waiting for them in outdoor Wyoming. It would be nice to think future generations will still hear the old-time phrase, "Well, kid, are you ready to go to the hills?"

Jay Lawson
North Fork Shoshone River
March 25, 2007

The author (right) and his sister, Leslie,
Evanston, Wyoming, 1952

About the Author

Jay Lawson has worked for the Wyoming Game and Fish Department for thirty years. He began his career as a game warden, was then promoted to the position of Regional Wildlife Supervisor, and later became Chief Game Warden and Chief of the Wildlife Division, a position he has held for eighteen years. Although wildlife management has been his lifelong career, his strong avocation is researching the history of the American West.

Jay wrote this book to preserve the life history of these fascinating men and women. In addition, he is donating all proceeds from the book to the Wildlife Heritage Foundation of Wyoming to further The Forensics Fund. This fund supports the forensic investigation of wildlife crimes by the Wyoming Game and Fish Department's laboratory at the University of Wyoming.

Photo courtesy of Mark Gocke

Wyoming Outdoor Timeline

1807   John Colter explores the Yellowstone area

1812   Robert Stuart discovers South Pass across the Rockies

1823   Sewel Newhouse patents the steel trap

1825   First Mountain Man Rendezvous

1834   William Sublette and Robert Campbell establish Fort William (later Fort Laramie)

1843   Scout Jim Bridger establishes Fort Bridger

1868   Wyoming becomes a territory

1869   Unlawful to sell big game from February 1 through August 1. First closed season on upland game birds from February 1 through August 15

1872   Yellowstone becomes the first national park

1873   Cheyenne Leader reports 200,000 buffalo had been slaughtered by rapacious market hunters

1875   First hunting season on big game from August 15 through January 15

1879   Legislators appoint the first State Fish Commissioner

First closure on beaver trapping for three years

1881   20,000 deer hides and 53,000 antelope hides shipped down the Yellowstone River

1883   Colonel William D. Pickett kills 4 grizzly bears on the Greybull River. His post office address "Four Bears, Wyoming" was named after the event

1884   First fishing season dates were set (June 1 through November 1)

1886   First bag limit placed on big game animals

1888   George Bird Grinnell and Colonel William D. Pickett are elected members of the new Boone and Crockett Club. They appoint noted gunslinger and plainsman Jim Gehman as Special Game Constable for what was then Fremont County. In his first year of appointment, one poacher attempts to shoot it out with the constable; Gehman kills him on the spot

Nonresident hunters are banned from Wyoming

1889   Last wild buffalo outside of Yellowstone National Park are killed north of Rawlins

1890   Wyoming becomes the 44th state on July 10

1895   Sale of game meat is outlawed altogether

        First Wyoming state game preserve is established

1899   First license required for residents (Gun license-$1.00) First creel limit on fish is adopted

        Office of State Game Warden is created by the legislature. Albert Nelson is appointed to fill that position.

        First closed season on moose

1902   First year big game licenses were required

1904   Antelope population is very low and "decreasing rapidly"

1906   President Theodore Roosevelt makes Devil's Tower the first national monument

1909   First closed season on antelope

        All wildlife declared to be the property of the state

1911   First Wyoming State Game Commission is created

        First provisions made for feeding wildlife

1923   First systematic effort to census all game animals

1929   Grand Teton becomes a national park

1937   Game and Fish Commission is granted authority over all wildlife matters by the legislature

        Dr. John W. Scott, Department of Zoology, University of Wyoming, takes a 2-year leave of absence to become Game and Fish Director

1939   Earl Durand of Powell is arrested for killing elk out of season. Hits jailer over the head with milk bottle and escapes. Last public posse in America is assembled for manhunt. A total of 6 people will die in subsequent gun battles including a major shoot-out near Clarks Fork Canyon. Durand's last act is an attempt to rob the Powell Bank. He is surrounded by locals with their hunting rifles. As Durand leaves the bank, a young teller he is using for a shield is killed. Seventeen year old Tipton Cox, a Powell high school junior, shoots Durand. Durand crawls back into the bank and kills himself. The event will be later featured in several motion pictures and books.

1945   Game wardens Don Simpson and Bill Lakanen are murdered by a poacher in the Sierra Madre mountains

1947   Commission establishes game management units

1949   Winter storms are the most severe on record. Due to high levels of mortality, the Red Desert is closed to antelope hunting

1955   The first open season for the hunting of wild turkeys occurs in the Black Hills

1961   Mule deer are extremely abundant, and the estimated harvest for this year is 84,677 animals

1962   The National Park Service begins direct reduction of elk in Yellowstone through shooting. The program is later halted due to extreme public opposition

1963   Trout are planted in the new Flaming Gorge Reservoir. 90,000 fishermen days are expected annually

1968   Elk are transplanted from Yellowstone National Park to the Ferris Mountains, Laramie Peak, Rawhide Buttes and the southern Big Horn Mountains

1972   Bighorn sheep are released in the Encampment River Canyon

1973   All game and fish laws are recodified

1975   Grizzly bears south of the Canadian border are classified as "threatened" under the Endangered Species Act

1978   Graduate student Beth Williams identifies Chronic Wasting Disease (CWD). She will later become a research veterinarian in Wyoming and a world authority on the disease

1980   A major pipeline breaks, spilling 8,000 barrels of crude oil into the North Platte River

1981   Peregrine falcon reintroduction begins, with 11 birds released into the wild

       The black-footed ferret, thought to be extinct, is rediscovered near Meeteetse

1987   Antelope are transplanted to the Wind River Indian Reservation to begin rebuilding their population

1988   Mountain lions are now abundant in the Big Horn Mountains, and domestic sheep losses are escalating

1991   The Wyoming Game and Fish Commission prevails in major litigation over the introduction of exotic species. Those species that pose any threat to native wildlife are not allowed

1992   The Wyoming Game and Fish Department develops model regulations governing the importation of wildlife. Species which could hybridize with native species, compete with native species, or pose a disease or parasite threat may not be imported or possessed

1995   The reintroduction goal of 30 nesting pairs of peregrine falcons is attained

The federal government releases 14 gray wolves in Yellowstone National Park

1999   Wyoming's bald eagle population increases to 85 nesting pairs

2003   Persistent drought results in low reservoir levels and reduced fishing and boating opportunities

Brucellosis is detected in a cattle herd near Pinedale, and this outbreak results in extensive negotiations and management planning for nearby elk herds that carry the disease. The pursuant agreement includes provisions for a pilot test and removal project for elk

2004   West Nile Virus is detected in numerous bird species, with significant mortality occurring among some sage grouse and raptor populations

Grizzly bear abundance and distribution has increased greatly and 134 human/grizzly conflicts are investigated this year

Renowned Wyoming wildlife veterinarians Beth Williams and Tom Thorne are killed in a tragic car accident

2005   Black-footed ferrets persist at the Shirley Basin reintroduction site with 89 ferrets being detected

2006   Wyoming files notice of intent to sue over the United States Fish and Wildlife Service's finding on the state's petition to delist the gray wolf

2007   The federal government attempts to remove the grizzly bear from the endangered species list

Photo courtesy of Wyoming Game and Fish Department

Thank you for your purchase of *Men To Match Our Mountains*, the proceeds of which will be donated by the author to the Wildlife Heritage Foundation's Forensics Fund. The fund directly supports the forensic unit at the Wyoming Game and Fish Department's laboratory, housed at the University of Wyoming.

Wyoming's forensic laboratory is one of the finest in the country and has received national recognition for its outstanding investigations. During the past two years, the lab assisted with 182 investigations, conducting tests on animal carcasses, tissue, blood, hair, antlers, saws, knives, gloves, jackets, fur, hide, teeth, arrows, bones, horns, hatchets, blankets, skulls and entrails. These cases resulted in fines totaling $278,229 in addition to jail and prison sentences and revoked hunting privileges. Examinations are also conducted on a contract basis for surrounding states, with Montana, Colorado, Utah, New Mexico and Utah depending entirely on our lab.

     The bottom line is—your purchase of this book will help us protect wildlife in Wyoming and throughout the Northern Rockies.

     The Wildlife Heritage Foundation of Wyoming is an independent, apolitical nonprofit corporation under the laws of the State of Wyoming. Their purpose is to provide financial support, through philanthropy, to critical wildlife conservation efforts in Wyoming. The Foundation's mission is to create an enduring natural legacy for future generations through stewardship of all Wyoming's wildlife.

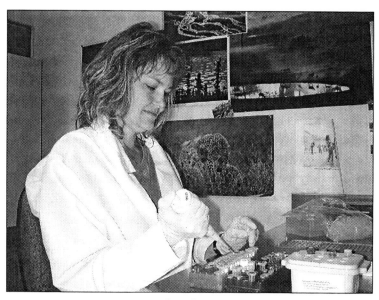

DeeDee Hawk, Labratory Director.

Kim Sargeant, Forensic Program Manager.

Printed in the United States
90752LV00003B/13-21/A

9 781932 636321